THE OXFORD GROUP

The Oxford Group

Its History and Significance

Walter Houston Clark

BOOKMAN ASSOCIATES : NEW YORK

Acknowledgment is made to the following publishers for permission to quote from their copyrighted works:

G. P. Putnam's Sons—H. Begbie, *More Twice-Born Men.*
Mackinac Press—F. N. D. Buchman, *Remaking the World.*
The Atlantic Monthly—H. P. Van Dusen, "Apostle to the Twentieth Century."
Dodd, Mead & Company—Henry Drummond, *The New Evangelism.*
Charles Scribner's Sons—D. C. Macintosh, *Personal Religion.*

Designed by Fred Kleeberg

MANUFACTURED IN THE UNITED STATES OF AMERICA

To E. H. C. and R. O'B. C.,
who in different ways contributed to the writing of this book.

Preface

THIS BOOK HAS been prepared with the idea that there was a need for a full-length study of the Oxford Group, or Moral Re-Armament. This movement is not only attempting to influence individuals but through these individuals to leave its mark on religious life, labor relations, international relations, and political movements. Legislative bodies and statesmen not only in the United States but throughout the world have received its attentions. Consequently it might seem that people interested in such affairs would welcome objective and systematic information about the Group. The book will also be of interest to students of contemporary social and religious history as well as to psychologists and other social scientists.

I have referred to my study as "objective." I am well aware that no study in the social, scientific, or religious field can be completely objective. What I mean is that I write from no partisan point of view. Doubtless on this account my book may be looked on by both the more extreme Groupists and their implacable enemies as highly unsatisfactory. But I have made an honest effort to understand the Group sympathetically, to do justice to its many undoubtedly creative contributions and insights at the same time that I have tried to point out what would seem to be its less evident weaknesses. Though never a member, I have followed the Group closely ever since I first attended, about 1924, some of its meetings for college students and met its leader.

The basis of this book is a doctoral dissertation presented at Harvard University. The latter has been rewritten in large part and expanded, both in order to increase its scope and to remove the Ph.D. curse with respect to its readability. The title of the initial study is *The Oxford Group: Its Work in American Colleges and its Effect on Participants.* Those who are interested in the documentation of material presented in the present volume or who would like to consult an extensive bibliography on the subject are referred to it. This exists only in manuscript and copies of it are on file at the Harvard University Library and also at the Library of the United States Office of Education in Washington, D.C. Ordinarily, these copies are available for inter-library loan.

The following pages contain a history of the movement, an inquiry into its religious origins and the character of its leader, Dr. F. N. D. Buchman, and a psychological study of its effects on people. The latter would seem to be a unique attempt to obtain objective information on what the religious experience fostered by the Group does to people, whether its effects are good or bad, and how lasting they are.

I am particularly indebted to Professor Gordon W. Allport of Harvard University, who first encouraged me to develop my interest in psychology and religion into a doctoral study of the Group and who has been most generous of his time in giving me suggestions and criticisms particularly with respect to the psychological aspects of that work; and to Professor Robert Ulich, also of Harvard, whose sympathetic guidance throughout the writing of the earlier study did much toward making it possible.

Were it not for my promise to keep their names in confidence, I would like to list the fifty-five people, later to be mentioned, who filled out the questionnaire concerning their experience with the Group, and who in a very real sense were collaborators in the study. Mrs. Virginia D. Thompson of the Penn State Christian Association kindly arranged to lend me valuable documents concerning Dr. Buchman's career at State College, Pennsylvania, and went to the trouble to discover persons there who could give me firsthand information. The staff at the Hartford Seminary Foundation were most cooperative not only in allowing me to see material in their files relating to Dr. Buchman and in giving me accounts of his career there, but also in locating material in the library which was not available elsewhere.

There are other individuals whom I would like to mention by name because they made available certain documents or information, read or criticized parts of my manuscripts, or gave me other special help. They are: Rev. A. Graham Baldwin, Rev. Henry M. Bartlett, Mrs. Kenneth D. Beckwith, E. M. Best, formerly President of Springfield College, Rev. E. Fay Campbell, Rev. Sherwood S. Day, the Honorable C. J. Hambro, Dr. Edgerton McC. Howard, Rev. F. C. Lawrence, the Honorable H. Alexander Smith, Mr. Edward Steese, Dr. and Mrs. Anson Phelps Stokes, and Mrs. Charles E. Sherman, who typed the manuscript.

This study is one that has required to a high degree the cooperation of other persons. Many hours of conference, criticism, or correspondence have been contributed by people other than those mentioned above whose friendship for me, interest in the subject, or simple courtesy has impelled them to give their help. One of the keenest pleasures in what has been a very pleasurable labor has been the opportunity to meet, even though often only by correspondence, scores of men and women whose interest in religious values or intellectual pursuits has been a stimulus and encouragement to me at the same time that I received more concrete help at their hands. I am sorry that they are too numerous for me to name individually, but I would like in this way at least to express my gratitude.

WALTER HOUSTON CLARK

Middlebury College
June, 1950

Contents

PART IV

EXPLANATION AND APPRAISAL

THE OXFORD GROUP

Chapter 1

Introduction

On a night in December, 1921, the Extension Lecturer in Personal Evangelism at Hartford Seminary lay in his Pullman berth. He was riding in the direction of his destination at Washington where he was to meet important people, delegates to the World Disarmament Conference. The delegates would come from many distant lands, especially from England and other parts of Europe where the Lecturer had often visited. Afflicted as he had always been with the "itching foot," the Lecturer needed little stimulus to set his thoughts wandering to foreign scenes, but on this particular night there was more point and direction than usual in his ruminations. He was thinking of the unsatisfactory nature of his position at Hartford, the altercations with the faculty and some of the student body, the humdrum nature of many of his duties, the confinement of his boarding-house room, and the obvious contempt in which he was held by some of his more scholarly colleagues. Of course they did not openly express this contempt to him, but the Lecturer was psychic, and no one on the faculty was his peer when it came to knowing what went on in other people's minds. True, there were compensations. The prestige of his connection with Hartford opened many doors to him; the Seminary was very generous with leaves of absence for his evangelistic work and even gave him an expense account for it (though it was never as large as he would have liked). Furthermore, he had made some converts on the campus, and his classes gave him an opportunity to touch the minds of young men and women in training for religious work and so expand his influence manyfold. For his courses were practical and vital, not stodgy and academic like the courses of his colleagues, who merely stuffed the minds of their students with data and left the person himself unchanged. But above all, the job offered him security, and a man—even an evangelist—needs to live on something. Yet what was that security worth to him if it prevented him from fulfilling his destiny? More and more the Lecturer was feeling hampered and cramped by his colleagues and the authorities at Hartford, and in proportion as he felt hemmed in and constrained, it was being borne upon him that what he needed was freedom, and that his mission was to convert the world.

But the Lecturer was not one to make decisions alone, or even to make them at all, if they were important. During many years he had schooled himself to listen for the decisions that God made for him. The hard thing was not so much to get messages from God as it was to summon the will to put the decisions into action, once the message was received. His decision boiled down to whether or not, like the Apostle Paul, he was to be obedient to the heavenly vision and give up his comfortable position to embark on uncharted seas. As he thought on and on, all the other considerations faded into the background or were lost in the misty regions of his unconscious as his thoughts focused more and more on this one issue: should he keep his job, or should he risk all his energies in the cause of world revival? Before he got off the train he must have a "quiet time" in which to listen once again for God's message.

When the Lecturer arrived in Washington the next morning, his decision had been made. And so, psychologically speaking, was born the Oxford Group, for the Lecturer was none other than the Reverend Frank Nathan Daniel Buchman, founder of the Group; and the decision, though it may have wavered somewhat in the meantime, was acted upon two months later. The Group itself prefers to date its beginning from the conversion of the first Oxford students by Buchman, and so far as its claim to its name goes, its preference is shrewd. But the importance of Buchman himself in the movement is so overwhelming that developments within the mind of the man himself have more significance than particular events; and more than any other one happening, it was the decision to leave Hartford that launched Buchman on his unique career.

As the beginning of the Group movement, the decision made in that sooty Pullman car has another appropriateness. This is that it was made in the United States. Since that time Dr. Buchman has become a citizen of the world, but the roots of the movement, as this book will show, are predominantly American, not English. However desirable it may be from the Group's point of view to represent itself as an Oxford product, the reader who wishes to understand the Group by learning about its origins must focus his gaze principally on the American scene. Though this is not the whole picture, nevertheless it is a very important part of the picture, and so the present volume will be concerned very largely with matters on the American side of the Atlantic.

Because even in the minds of many otherwise well-informed people the Oxford Group is identified with the Oxford Movement, it is appropriate here at the beginning to clarify this issue. The Oxford Movement was a really indigenous Oxford development of well over a century ago which involved John Henry Newman and others in their efforts to Catholicize the Anglican church. The effects of the movement are now represented in that communion by the High Church wing, often referred to as Anglo-Catholic, with its emphasis on liturgical tradition and dogma. The Oxford Group movement, on the contrary, is basically evangelical, with the emphasis on the conversion of the individual and the training of the will. By keeping away from dogma or any set liturgy the Oxford Group has managed to adapt itself to many different types of faith, Christian and non-Christian. Delegates from Japan, Brazil, Egypt, Ceylon, Indonesia, Afghanistan, and Pakistan recently attended a worldwide conference sponsored by the Group at Caux, Switzerland. Roman Catholics, both clerics and laymen, have attended and endorsed its work. Only convinced Communists are unwelcome. Anyone who acknowledges a Higher Power or whose mind is open to the possibility of such a Power, and who is willing to give the message of the Group a hearing, is welcome at its councils. But its face is set like flint against the doctrines of the Kremlin.

Furthermore the Group represents religion that is alive. William James speaks of individuals "for whom religion exists not as a dull habit, but as an acute fever." This description aptly characterizes the typical Groupist. As a matter of fact, the chief function of the group is to raise the individual's religious temperature, and if this temperature becomes too high for some, while in others it burns itself out too quickly, this is not to gainsay the evidence that for many persons the Group has fanned the dead embers of a merely verbalized religion into a flame, while for some individuals it has performed what has amounted to a life-saving operation on the personality. Our account of the Group will include the stories of a number of persons with varied experiences which will document this statement.

Yet the purpose of this book is not to be the glorification of the Oxford Group. Anybody can find all the glory he wants in the highly colored accounts written by such journalistic converts as A. J. Russell, Victor Kitchen, Peter Howard, or contributors to the *New World News,* the Groupist newspaper. For the followers of the Oxford Group are like those of any other vital religious movement; they are sincerely convinced that the secret of the solution of all political ills is theirs. Did I say spiritual ills? Nay, economic and political ills as well. Change the individual, teach him to listen for God's guidance and to follow it: this is what every person needs and what will change the world. In this way will come the end of political bickerings, for it will cease to matter whether one lives in a democracy or a dictatorship. Gone will be the strife between capital and labor, for labor boss and cartel magnate will lie down together like lambs. Teach the secret of God guidance, and thus will be solved "every last bewildering problem." The only thing we need to beware is a person or a system who teaches us that there is no God to guide. Thus we can understand Buchman's keen nose for the smokes of hell-fire smouldering in the heart of Communism, though he hardly saw it when it blazed from the eyes of Hitler.

And so it is that the objective person is bewildered as he approaches the Oxford Group. At one time he is amazed at the spiritual miracle wrought in some sour-minded, wrongheaded individual; at another he is repelled by the upstart arrogance and spiritual pride of a newly converted youngster; at times he is shocked by the political and theological naïveté of the leader's views on world problems; at other times he senses in the very simplicity of these views a perception of values for lack of which our civilization may very well go down to destruction. The Oxford Group has demonstrated that it has the power to touch men's hearts and to change their lives. Should we scorn it and reject it as a whole simply because we may suspect some of its methods or dislike some of its manifestations?

But whatever one's attitude may be, there is no doubt that the Group—or Moral Re-Armament, its current title in world councils—is beginning to be a force to be reckoned with. It has had its ups and downs in the past. Like Wall Street it has had its bull markets and its bear markets; and also, like Wall Street, its long-term trend seems to be upward. Just now one of its periodic recessions seems to have ended, and it is once more on the move. It has had the comfort and endorsement, if not the actual adherence, of many prominent men and women, among them not a few world leaders. Emil Brunner, noted Swiss theologian, has written about the Group endorsing its work and is reported to be a member; while Robert Schuman, French Foreign Minister, sent a keynote message to a recent world gathering at Caux and has promised to attend a meeting there in the early future. Other figures prominent in European affairs have had similar relations with the Group. In the United States also the Group has been active in making friends for its cause in high places. President Truman is among those who have given their blessing to its work. Admiral Byrd is a member. Many Senators and Congressmen have been more or less closely associated with its program, while recently the House of Representatives has been persuaded to vote an appropriation to send some of its members as official delegates to Caux. It is important that we define our attitude toward this movement, which for good or ill intends to have some influence not only on the religious life of the time but on the affairs of nations.

But in order that our estimate of the Group may be fair and sound it is important first that we *understand* it. This was the thesis of the study of which this book is the record, and it is the aim of the book to help the reader sympathetically yet critically to acquire the important information about the Group. Though the writer will be frank about his opinions and surreptitiously hopes that the reader will agree with him, nevertheless he is going to try to make his presentation sufficiently objective so that the main burden of forming an opinion will fall on the reader.

Evidence of several different varieties will be introduced. The main framework of the book will be the story of the Group, starting with the early history of Dr. Buchman, and emphasizing the beginnings of the Group in the United States, but carrying on the account until present times. Those who are mainly interested in this aspect of the book should concentrate on Part One. Part Two will embody treatment of Dr. Buchman's personality and the influences in his background that help to explain the features and practices of the Group. Part Three tells the story of the experiences that different persons have had with the Group.

The whole, but principally Part Four, will contain an account of strengths and weaknesses, successes and failures, criticisms and appreciations. One of the characteristics of Dr. Buchman and his movement, from the earliest records which we have been able to find, is the extreme partisanship with which they have always been surrounded. The whole subject is one where most people have difficulty in seeing anything but black or white. While this has made for lively reading in some of the sources, it has not always led to clarity. The reader will not find that extreme partisanship, either pro or con, in these pages. Consequently they will doubtless appeal to more forthright intellects as but insipid reading. But for those whose judgments are more tempered, who are willing to reserve decisions until evidence has been presented, this book will try to present both sides.

After all, the Oxford Group and Moral Re-Armament, like all other movements both secular and religious, are the products of human personality. Personality, needless to say, is not only fallible but infinitely complex. It is hardly likely that the movement created out of the interaction of myriads of complex personalities will be less difficult to understand and appraise than the individuals out of which it grew.

PART I

Story of the Oxford Group

Chapter Two

What Is the Oxford Group?

RELIGION HAS TWO characteristic expressions, the professional and non-professional. The Oxford Group from its very beginning has self-consciously striven to be non-professional or lay in its emphasis. This has sometimes disturbed those to whom religion is an orderly and traditional affair; occasionally it has even infuriated some ecclesiastical watch-dogs and preservers of churchly prerogative. However, it would seem that if one is to object to the Oxford Group, it must be on better ground than this. For most religious movements have owed their religious impulse to laymen. The Wesleyan movement and the Quakers illustrate this truth. The Hebrew prophets were mostly laymen, while a large proportion of the Christian martyrs and saints of the Church themselves were lay people. One might even reflect on a certain Carpenter, the Foundation on which most of our ecclesiastical machinery is laid, Who was not only a layman Himself but chose no single ecclesiastic among His twelve immediate followers.

And it is this Carpenter that Frank Buchman has striven to imitate and follow. How successful he has been, of course, is for the individual student to determine for himself. As a matter of fact it is one of the questions under consideration in this book; but of the fundamental sincerity of Buchman's attempt there is little doubt. Equally clear is the fact that it is the layman who has played the prominent part in the movement from the beginning. Even where professional religious people have been admitted, they have brought no part of the ecclesiastical apparatus with them. Buchman himself is an ordained Lutheran minister, but this connection has played no important role in the performance of what he considers his God-directed task. As will be specified in more detail in later chapters, the Oxford Group started as a student movement, counterparts for which can be found in the annals of many colleges and universities both in America and abroad.

Yet one must not get the impression from the foregoing that church people have been invariably hostile to the Oxford Group, for in fact many have warmly welcomed its work and its ministrations as a powerful, vital influence in modern religious life. The Group claims to be neither a church nor a religious institution and tries to stay off denominational preserves by using no influence to stimulate change of membership from one type of religious faith to another. Its techniques can be adapted to vitalize the members of any religious faith. Perhaps the best way to describe the situation is to say that institutional membership is simply extraneous to the Oxford Group. It makes no difference whether the person is Protestant or Catholic, a good church member or a poor one, a Christian or a pagan. All of this is in spite of the fact that the roots of the movement and its leadership have been Christian, Protestant, and evangelical.

The aims and the methods of the Oxford Group have remained essentially the same since the early 1920's, though emphases have changed somewhat through the years. The techniques of the Group have their counterparts in other religious movements both current and historic. Most distinguishing are not so much the techniques themselves as the terms used to describe them. Like most self-conscious groups of whatever variety, the Oxford Group has its own technical jargon. The first thing that the neophyte convert does is to learn these terms, and since the Group eschews such conventionalities as membership lists and disclaims the possibility of any such conventional process as "joining," the best method available for determining who "belongs" to the Group and who does not is to note whether a person talks the Group "language." Consequently it is important to understand the most important of these terms. In addition it will be convenient to describe the main features of Group technique and emphasis in connection with the terms.

The Changed Life. The central focus of Group endeavor is the "changed" life. "Change" is simply the Group term for conversion, the reorientation of the individual toward a better life. The Group sees its world mission in terms of changing people rather than in changing political situations, the social structure, or economic systems. This is one cardinal issue on which the Group differs from Communism. But this also tends to separate the Groupists from fellow Christians who emphasize the Social Gospel as well as from the typical liberal and the non-communist socialist. This also helps to explain why the Oxford Group readily finds a warm spot in the hearts of many conservatives and those whose vested interests lie in the preservation of the *status quo*. This is not to say that there have not been many liberals who have seen great value in its program and some who have joined the movement. Neither should one get the impression that its conservative supporters are not sincere. To read certain liberal journals is to get the impression that the Oxford Group and Moral Re-Armament is one great plot to impose on the little man and perpetuate capitalism. An acquaintance with any of the leaders of the Group will convince any fair-minded person of their sincerity. It is simply ideologically easier for conservatives to accept the Group program; but that the movement may be used as a tool of special interests is a danger concerning which the Group should indeed be more alert than apparently it is.

The stages involved in the process of changing the individual used to be partly listed by Buchman as "Confidence, Confession, Conviction, Conversion, and Continuance," a prescription often offered to attendants at his early meetings. "Confidence" involved the establishment of rapport by the "life changer" with the sinner, or person to be changed; practically speaking, any person outside of the Group. "Confession" involved the confession of sins either in public or in private. In earlier days there was more public confession than at present, for meetings were smaller then; besides, painful experience has taught the Group that public confession is not always wise even though it may have a very beneficial effect on the individual. However, a certain type of confession, known as "sharing for witness," is still practiced. This is the confession of faults long since overcome by a "changed" individual for the purpose of encouraging prospective converts. "Conviction" was that mental process by which the "unchanged" became aware of his sinfulness. It was always assumed that everyone had some fault or sin of which he could be made ashamed; but this shame was not regarded as an end in itself but simply as a necessary preliminary to the changed life on a higher and more satisfactory plane. "Conversion" was the change itself, that act of will in which one definitely promised oneself, God, or another person that he would forsake his sins and follow God's "Guidance." Not even a prior belief in God was strictly necessary. To act *as if* there were a God was sufficient; a genuine belief in God frequently followed the assumption through this pragmatic process. "Continuance" involved the activity which strengthened and confirmed conversion through seeking and following "Guidance," and usually consisted in "changing" others as well as other acts of well-doing.

The "five C's" are not spoken about today at Group meetings as much as they used to be, but they still outline pretty accurately what is involved in life-changing.

Guidance and the *Quiet Time*. A concept equal in importance to the "changed life" is that of Guidance. So far as the Group has any central dogma it is that God will give guidance to those who listen for it with the sincere intent to put it into practice. Of course, as any Christian will hold, it needs no ghost come from the grave to reveal this piece of theology, and neither Buchman nor the Group will maintain that they have originated the concept. But it is the emphasis on it that is characteristic. "Everyone can listen to God." "The only sane people in an insane world are those guided by God." "Definite direction, accurate information can still come from the Mind of God to the mind of man." "If we do not listen to guidance, we must listen to guns." Statements like the foregoing can be found in nearly all Buchman's public addresses, usually repeated many times over. Furthermore the burden of the message is the same today as it was twenty years ago. Consequently a most important part of the Group program involves techniques for securing God's guidance.

The chief technique to this end is what the Group calls the "Quiet Time." This is simply the term given to the period for meditation, which is carried out sometimes by individuals, but often in groups. Most Oxford Group gatherings will involve at least one Quiet Time during the program when people are encouraged to take pencils and notebooks in order to jot down what "comes to them." Dr. Buchman makes a great point of what he calls "two-way prayer," which involves listening to God as well as speaking to Him, and it is usually implied that the listening aspect is the more important. What "comes to" the listeners ranges all the way from profound spiritual insights and self-revelations to absurd trivialities. One man may be guided to apologize and make restitution to a business rival whom he has wronged, while another may receive a message to sell his hundred shares of Union Pacific. An observer who listens to the process of the "sharing" of guidance, which usually follows the Quiet Time, will be struck by the fact that much of the guidance related will be of a very obvious and commonplace character. At one very large and public meeting a person got up with the "guidance" to read a very long and tedious poem. The moderator of the meeting apparently had received contrary directions, and the ensuing altercation was hardly an edifying spectacle for the rest of those present. Another member of the Group found a premium coming due on his insurance policy, his only monetary asset. He was "guided" to share his financial worries with another wealthier member, with the result that the premiums for the next five years were paid for him.

The Group is far from being unaware of such absurdities and anomalies, and the warning is often voiced that not everything that appears to be guidance comes from God. To guard against unwise action—for many foolish things have been done which purported to be the will of God—the Group has developed the practice of "checking" guidance. This is the submission of guidance to the judgment of the other Group members for advice. Also no guidance is looked on as genuine which violates the standards of the "Four Absolutes," to be described next.

The Four Absolutes. The ethical program of the Group is epitomized in the counsel of moral perfection defined by the Four Absolutes of perfect honesty, purity, unselfishness, and love. These standards not only serve to provide control for the concept of guidance, but they serve as a means whereby the individual may test his life and develop a program for individual or for public improvement. The Four Absolutes have been featured in most of the Group's plays and programs, and along with Guidance and Change have been a powerful influence in the lives of many individuals.

The Houseparty. The nearest counterpart to the Oxford Group "Houseparty" is what a Catholic would call a "retreat" and a Protestant would call a "conference." Though it has some of the features of each, it is probably closer in spirit to the latter. Houseparties are now neither so common nor as well publicized as they were in earlier days, but the term is still sometimes used, and they were most important in the development of the movement. Originally they were often held in a private home, hence the name, which also happened to imply the informality which Buchman was always careful to have as a feature of those meetings. As the work grew, houseparties were held at hotels, or country inns where distractions were at a minimum and where large rooms were available for meetings. Those attending paid their own expenses, which were often high; though in certain cases the expenses were borne by organizations, such as college Christian associations, or even occasionally underwritten personally by Dr. Buchman himself. Here the process of guidance, quiet times, "sharing," fellowship, and life-changing went forward under the sensitive and skillful direction of the leader.

In recent times the term Houseparty has been applied to the mass gatherings held by the Group in different parts of the world—such as the "International House Party" of July, 1934, held at Oxford—very different in scope from the modest meetings of thirty to forty people of the early 1920's. Today the large meetings for Moral Re-Armament are more appropriately called "Assemblies," though many of their features, in particular their informality, gaiety, and good spirits, they owe to the Houseparty of earlier times.

It is very difficult for a person who never attended one of the early houseparties to do justice to its atmosphere, the distinctive element of these meetings. Confidences on the part of those attending were encouraged by various means, and both public and private confessions, sometimes of a very intimate character, were elicited. Since many of these were of a sexual nature, there was considerable criticism by outsiders. Some of these criticisms were undoubtedly justified, for some harm was done. In general, however, the results were personally beneficial, and participants at these meetings, particularly when conducted by Buchman in person, testify to the skill and propriety with which they were handled. A later chapter contains a firsthand account of a typical early houseparty written by a person who had attended several of these meetings.

Key men and the *Team.* While not given prominence in the literature, the term "key men" is often heard in the counsels of the Group. Dr. Buchman, or "Frank," as he is always known to his followers, always made special efforts to convert the leaders in any group on which he had designs on the sound theory that the prestige of such people would enable them to touch others and so to spread the influence of the movement.

He would then attempt to persuade the most impressive of these key men to accompany him on his evangelical trips. This group would be known as the "team." In the early days of the movement the members of teams were usually young men in college or recent graduates. Athletes or other such leaders on college campuses were especially prized as team members. It was Buchman's habit to remain in the background at meetings as much as possible, calling on the team members and others to do the talking. Many times attendants at houseparties brought away a much more vivid remembrance of team members than of Buchman himself. Membership in a team did not always signify complete dedication to the movement, but a place was often offered to "key men" who were thought to be on the road to conversion because their participation was likely to speed the process. This latter motive also operated in the encouragement of participation at meetings on the part of the rank and file.

Today the activities of teams and the interest in key people are as green as in days gone by. But instead of an interest in a football captain or president of the student body, the modern quarry is a foreign minister or the head of a state; instead of a team visit to a neighboring campus, a modern team may circle the globe.

Living on Faith. A small minority of the specially dedicated among the Group, led by the example of Buchman himself, "live on faith," by which is meant that they rely on God to guide others to take care of their material needs. There has been some criticism of the Group on account of this, and there is even occasionally heard the suggestion that it is a kind of money-making racket. There is no evidence whatsoever that this is the case. The Group prides itself on never asking for funds, and this claim is honest so far as direct appeals go. It is possible that there may be an element of pharasaical boasting about the contention. Like any movement, the Group needs funds, and it would be hard to say that its well-known interest in the wealthy as well as the prominent has no element in it of concern for the material well-being of the movement and those whom it supports. The story, mentioned above, of the young man who got his insurance policy paid, suggests practices that could lend themselves to abuses. Also there are some evangelists who could not travel in the sumptuous fashion that characterizes the trips of Dr. Buchman without a twinge of conscience. However, that gentleman apparently never questions the propriety of lavish expenditures when the money is there and the cause is a good one. Living on faith has not always been an easy adventure, and he has known what it means not to know from whence his next meal was coming; but he has always been sure that "where God guides, He provides," and that "good Christians and good living go together."

While he never asks for funds directly, he has developed skill in putting his message so compellingly and so skillfully that people are impelled to give. Sometimes it may be a hint after "guidance" that a wealthy member might find it possible to underwrite a project; or just the right compliment to a wealthy dowager may result in a donation; or an expression of thanks for funds in a prayer may suggest to people that the material needs of the members must be cared for in some way.

In addition to this, Dr. Buchman has never been very meticulous in accounting for funds that are given to him, despite the fact that some of his supporters advocated strict accounting as a safeguard against much unjustifiable criticism. He seems to have taken the position that guidance would always take care of the proper disposal of funds entrusted to him, and those who are close to him have always been certain that this has been the case. Recently, however, with the tremendous growth of the movement, more business-like practices have been introduced, so that this aspect of the criticism has less force than formerly.

Money, the Bible reminds us, is the root of all evil, and it would be strange if it exerted a less corrupting pressure on the Group than on other equally worthy movements. This pressure is not direct and obvious but indirect and subtle, so as to be ten times as dangerous. We may presume that sensitive consciences among the membership are aware that great temptation as well as great courage is involved in the process of living on faith.

Sharing. A final term much used by the Group is "sharing." Primarily, this refers to the confession of sins to one another, but it also refers to the exchange of guidance and other experiences of a religious or ethical nature. "Sharing for witness" has already been alluded to and denotes the confession of sins, long since committed and properly mastered, for the purpose of encouraging other sharing and to suggest to other people the possibility of a changed life. Sometimes this is the first step in establishing confidence in a person with difficulties similar to those described by the witness, and may lead to a rapport between two persons that not only effects "change" but leads to a friendship of a very lasting and satisfying type.

Sharing of these various types as well as many of the other activities described combine to make what is not so much in outward organization but rather in actual practice a closely-knit and very soul-satisfying fellowship. People come to know one another as they really are. Not only deeply hidden faults and frustrations but equally contained hopes and aspirations are laid open to other people who are similarly minded. This sense of fellowship is sometimes acutely accentuated by the frequent criticisms to which the Group is at times subjected. Jocosely, Buchman likes to refer to it as a "fellowship of sinners," and if this is so, then many come to find this consequence of sin a very pleasant thing. Certainly sharing and the resulting fellowship go far to explain psychologically much of the appeal of the Group.

The name "Oxford Group." The Oxford Group is peculiarly the product of its founder, Dr. Buchman, a man in no way connected with Oxford either officially, traditionally, or by habits of thinking. The early phase of his movement was known by the much more accurate but less impressive name "Buchmanism." Its adherents always disliked the term, and about 1927 they named themselves "A First Century Christian Fellowship." In 1928, when a "team" was touring South Africa, they were called the "Oxford Group," a name which met with instant favor among themselves. Just before World War II, the name Moral Re-Armament (MRA) has been acquired and used in connection with publicity and certain special projects. But under all these names the inspiration has come from Dr. Buchman and a small group of followers, some of whom have supported him since the early 1920's.

Chapter Three

Buchman's Start as an Evangelist

THE FAMILY OF Frank Buchman emigrated in 1740 from Switzerland to Pennsburg, Pennsylvania, where they remained nearly a hundred and fifty years. It is interesting to know that an ancestor, Bibliander, successor to Zwingli in the chair of theology at Zurich, used to invite students to his house to help them with their doubts and difficulties. It was at Pennsburg that Frank was born on June 4, 1878, to Frank and Sarah (Greenwalt) Buchman, simple, religious people typically "Pennsylvania Dutch." When the boy was fifteen, his parents moved to Allentown, Pennsylvania, where, according to the *Morning Call,* his father, a distiller, is still remembered as one of the city's "ethical business men, a Christian gentleman." From him his son acquired his understanding of human nature. His mother is described as a quiet, cultured woman of deep insight, rigidly self-disciplined but with a sense of humor. His upbringing was theologically conservative and pietistic, which would explain his sense of personal contact with God, his ideas of innate evil in man, and his belief in regeneration. His confirmation brought him no outstanding spiritual experience. He was graduated from the Allentown High School and entered Muhlenberg College, where he was reserved, reticent, and undistinguished. On graduation in 1899, he entered the Philadelphia Seminary (Lutheran) at Mt. Airy, from which he was graduated in 1902. In later years he received an honorary D. D. from Muhlenberg. A fellow student at the seminary had accused him of ambition, which disturbed him to such an extent that for his first charge he chose a very poor and difficult parish, the Church of the Good Shepherd, at Overbrook, Philadelphia; but first he spent a year of graduate study abroad. He studied at Westminster College (Presbyterian), Cambridge, and also at the Inner Mission in Germany. In Germany he also worked with Father Bodelschwingh at Bethel, and accompanied him on some of his journeys. The latter is said to have made a deep impression on him. He visited the Rauhe Haus in Hamburg and the Johannestift in Spandau, as well as Neuendettelsau, Gnadenthal, and Kaiserswerth. He learned from Stöcker and Le Seur and so, according to a German account of him, "drank from the best sources of our (German) social Christianity." Returning to America he took up his ministry at Overbrook, where his church consisted of a corner shop, his congregation largely of servants, recruited often by ringing doorbells at big houses. Influenced probably by his German contacts, he established a work place in an attic in a poor district in Philadelphia. Here the human derelicts and unfortunates who crowded around were not turned away. Along with comfort and understanding they received food and clothing, while Buchman learned that "where God guides, He provides." However, during this period he also spent some time at the dinner tables and in the homes of the wealthy, a habit afterward conspicuous in the work of the Oxford Group.

In 1905, Dr. Buchman founded what may have been the first Lutheran Hospice for young men in this country, and later a settlement house in Philadelphia. In this work he learned to handle boys and converted many; but in 1908 he had a falling out with the trustees who wished to balance the budget, while Buchman wanted to feed the hungry. As a result he resigned in a huff, nursing ill-will against the six trustees who had dominated him.

In poor health as the result of overwork, he left for England, where he attended the Keswick Conference in June. He was one day attending a tiny church there, when he heard a sermon on the Cross by a woman preacher. Suddenly he became convicted of sin—"selfishness, pride, ill-will"—and had a vision of the estranged Christ with "infinite suffering on the face of the Master." The realization of this estrangement and the sorrow of Christ, in the words of Begbie,

> . . . dissipated the chaos in his mind; there was now no hesitancy, no feeling of a divided will, no sense of calculation and argument; a wave of strong emotion, rising up within him from the depths of his estranged spiritual life, seemed, as it were, to lift his soul from its anchorage of selfishness and to bear it across that great sundering abyss to the foot of the Cross. There he made his surrender to the divine will; there he lost all sense of oppression and helplessness. It was the work of a moment, and a gesture of his spirit invisible to human eyes.
>
> I asked him to recall if he could the physical sensations of that moment of surrender. . . .
>
> He said, "I remember one sensation very distinctly; it was a vibrant feeling up and down the spine, as if a strong current of life had suddenly been poured into me. That followed on my surrender. No; it came at the same time. It was instantaneous."*

A sense of buoyancy came as the result of this, and he went back to the house where he was staying to write letters of apology to the six trustees. The resulting sense of relief and

* H. Begbie, *More Twice-Born Men* (New York, G. P. Putnam's Sons, 1923), pp. 24-25.

well-being made him tell the story to his hosts at tea, with the consequence that the son of the family was converted. Apparently, this introduced him to the value of confession for witness, or "sharing."

Some months later, in 1908, the Reverend Wellington H. Tinker was speaking to a group of medical students in Philadelphia. After the meeting, he was approached by one of the group who invited him to his room for a cup of tea. It was Mr. Buchman, returned from England, who stated that he wanted a position as a student Y.M.C.A. secretary. Mr. Tinker was a little skeptical about his qualifications, but suggested he write John R. Mott, then in charge of student work for the Y.M.C.A. Mr. Tinker later wrote to Mott about the young man, stressing his obvious sincerity. One informant states that Buchman asked Mott for the hardest student secretaryship available. If so, it follows the same pattern of his seeking a pastorate six years earlier. Shortly afterward H. P. Anderson of the Y.M.C.A. office in New York wrote Professor J. M. Willard, Chairman of the State College (Pennsylvania) Y.M.C.A. Advisory Committee, recommending Buchman for the position of college Y.M.C.A. secretary, and describing him as a "man of breadth, great personal attractiveness," and saying that he would recommend him elsewhere if Penn State was not interested. Apparently it was, for a subsequent letter from Buchman says he knows State College to be a "key position" and that he plans to visit. A letter in support of Buchman's candidacy from a minister who had lived at his hospice says "I can't but believe that he would be able to bring something to the work at State that it has not had before." The result of these negotiations was that Buchman was engaged as secretary of the State College Y.M.C.A. from January 1 to July 1, 1909, at a salary of $600 plus room, though the draft of a letter to Buchman indicates he was told that punctual payment might be difficult.

In this position his duties were to supervise and direct the activities of the College Christian association, to encourage membership, raise money for the association, recruit delegations for attendance at student conferences such as were held at Eagles Mere and Northfield, arrange meetings, and in general to stimulate student religious life in any way that seemed promising. His program was pretty well prescribed for him through the pattern of the conventional college Y.M.C.A. secretary; but, as will be shown, his work at Penn State was outstanding and original in several ways.

State College drew largely young men and women from the small towns and farms in Pennsylvania. The wealthier students of the state attended the better-known colleges in the East, such as Harvard, Yale, and Vassar, so that not much money was available on the campus to ease the way for money-raising; on the other hand, the college was isolated in a small community and the Christian association had little competition from the distractions that wealth might have provided. The college increased in members from six or seven hundred students when Buchman came, to well over twice the number before he left; but the Y.M.C.A. membership increased out of all proportion to enrollment. According to a rough graph in the files, membership in the Y comprised less than thirty-five per cent of the student body in 1907, while in 1911 it was better than seventy-five per cent. It is possible that the official figures may have been somewhat inflated. A complaining alumnus states that Buchman was in the habit of enrolling incoming freshmen in the Y on the strength of their accepting gift Bibles, and on the basis of this sent them bills for dues. However, students of those days in general confirm the Group literature to the effect that there was heightened religious activity and interest during Buchman's tenure.

Buchman seems to have been equally successful at money-raising, being very resourceful at bringing his work to the notice of those who had the wherewithal to finance it. As an example, there is the story of how he got money to send a large delegation from Penn State to one or more of the college conferences. Some of his helpers were sent with directions to gather for him large quantities of trailing arbutus. This was packed neatly in boxes and sent, with his card in each, to various well-known wealthy women, some of whom sent large checks for the work of the association. The result was that many students could be offered trips to the conferences with all expenses paid. At one conference, the Penn State delegation numbered over a hundred men. In such ways Buchman plumed his pride at the same time that he carried forward the work of the Kingdom.

He was similarly successful at organizing conferences and campaigns himself, where he showed a genius for the detail which work of this kind requires. One authority speaks of Buchman as having inaugurated at Penn State in 1915 the large-scale evangelistic campaigns, unique in the number of interviews arranged. He was a genius at introducing men to those who could be of the greatest help to them. He organized many voluntary Bible classes. In a letter to Henry B. Wright of Yale in the fall of 1909 he speaks of teaching three large classes on Sunday, while by the time he left there were said to be twelve hundred men doing voluntary Bible study in classes scattered over the campus. Apparently his main influence was with men rather than women, though he did have one Sunday Bible class for women into which he went for the first time "with fear and trembling."

Yet he was not only successful at big things but also in

smaller groups and in touching the lives of individuals. Every morning at five a small group gathered in his room for the "Morning Watch," as the later "Quiet Time" was then termed. Here reading of the Bible was followed by "listening to God," and plans for religious activities were made. He also held similar meetings on Sunday evenings at nine-thirty or ten. To such meetings came those whom he had successfully challenged to live lives on the basis of the highest that they knew, following standards of purity and honesty very similar to those that afterward became the "Four Absolutes." Such men were completely devoted to him, sometimes cutting short visits and coming miles to attend the Sunday meetings or rising from bed after shortened sleep to be at his room in the morning. His influence extended to the faculty and town, particularly after his conversion of the college bootlegger, "Bill Pickle," famous to all Groupists. An old resident of State College and minister of one of the churches there at the time writes that he feels that Buchman did a great Christian work and that his activities were not entirely confined to the campus. "He was indeed a man of single-eyed sincerity who achieved much. . . . In the town he devoted time and strength to personal work among people who were away from the regular church groups—people who are often referred to as underprivileged." It was his sound theory that converts needed activity and religious expression to maintain their conversions on the proper plane; consequently he was active in arranging not only trips to conferences but various constructive projects, such as campaigns in jails and reformatories to give the students a chance to help and convert the inmates.

While there were some minor frictions and misunderstandings with students and faculty, there do not appear to have been serious disagreements such as disturbed his relation with others at the Lutheran hospice or afterward at Hartford and at Princeton. However, there were some members of the faculty who disapproved of his activities and a number of students similarly disposed. His campus nickname, "Pure John," suggests a certain amount of ridicule, though apparently mingled with respect. While one student of that day states that Buchman was not highly respected by the rank and file, another says that despite the ridicule there was no one on the campus who would not have been embarrassed to be observed by Buchman indulging in some vice. While, as has already been indicated, he was interested in the welfare of the poor and unfortunate, his aim at Penn State was principally directed toward the leaders on the campus. In a letter to the evangelist, Henry Wright, he says, "We are after the key men and are getting them." In the same letter he asks Professor Wright to write congratulations to the Penn State football captain on his successful season, which shows what pains he took with those whom it was his desire to convert.

One very important contact made by Buchman at this time was with the same Henry Wright, professor at Yale, and one of the finest college evangelists of his day. He was very active at student conferences, where it is likely Buchman first came in contact with him. Buchman was greatly impressed by him, perhaps even idolized him. Wright came to Penn State numerous times on Buchman's invitation to carry on evangelistic work, and Buchman used Wright's religious manual in his Bible classes at this time. His influence on Buchman, and hence on the Group movement as a whole, was a very important one, and will be dealt with in Part II.

Some loose notes in the Penn State Christian Association files list some of the features of Buchman's methods at State College. They are "(1) appeal to the individual rather than the masses; (2) guidance by God in the ordinary affairs of life, i.e. in work, sleep, recreation, eating; (3) to make prayer not only a petition but also a surrender and a listening; (4) with no intelligent expressional activity for an emotion, it dies or shows itself in undesirable ways." If we add to these (5) the emphasis on winning leaders or "key men"; (6) shrewdness in approaching people able and willing to finance religious work; (7) conversion through a challenge to live a life based on moral absolutes; and (8) a close fellowship of converts strongly attached to him through personal loyalty, we can see the main features of the Oxford Group taking shape. Few if any of his early followers carried over into the Group proper, but State College was the laboratory in which the leader was testing his methods, crystallizing his ideas, and doing a prodigious amount of active work under the inspiration of his oft-quoted motto, "I can do all things through Christ, which strengtheneth me."

Chapter Four

Buchman at Hartford Seminary

Hartford Seminary, a small non-sectarian theological school at Hartford, Connecticut, has had an evangelical tradition and has always tried to have an active evangelist on its staff. In 1916 the President, the Reverend William D. Mackenzie, a man of broad religious sympathies, proposed to bring to the Seminary the most able evangelist available. At that time the Reverend Howard Walter, a graduate of the Seminary and former missionary to China, who was then assisting at a church in Hartford, recommended Buchman. The latter had resigned his work at State College in 1915 and spent a year in India, Korea, and Japan with the evangelist, Sherwood Eddy. Accordingly, the dean of the Seminary, the Reverend Melancthon C. Jacobus, who had made further investigation, recommended that Mr. Buchman be appointed for a year as Extension Lecturer in Personal Evangelism. It was understood that beside teaching, he would also have time free for actual evangelistic work in the field, for which he was given an expense account. This was justified in the eyes of the Trustees not only as a contribution to the wider Christian enterprise but as a means of making contacts with prospective students for the Seminary. Mr. Buchman was always very insistent on the prompt receipt of his checks, and the expense account was a source of some friction between him and the officers of the Seminary. It was probably in the Spring of 1916 when Buchman first took up his duties at Hartford, living at Hosmer Hall, the student dormitory, for the first year or two. His appointment as lecturer was renewed annually until his withdrawal in 1922. He was not a member of the governing faculty and was several times given long leaves of absence to pursue his evangelistic work.

The notices of his courses in the Foundation Bulletin do not yield much information about their content. However, a memorandum in the Foundation files on his courses for 1921-22 gives the following:

1. Beginning Course. Principles of Personal Evangelism (two classes—one for men and one for women).
2. Advanced Course. Diagnosis, Personalization, Illustration, Recent Movement at Oxford and Cambridge. Discourse different from Advanced course of last year.
3. Course for Bible and Personal Evangelism. Open to men and women. This course shows how to use the Bible in dealing with individuals, and shows how the Bible is the book for this age.
4. Clinic for men. Open to all men who are taking the course.

One former student who took a course with Dr. Buchman has a very hazy recollection of the content of the course but a strong remembrance of his impression that the teacher was anxious to convert each member of the class. Of the material covered, he recalls only that much was said of St. Augustine and the other Christian mystics. A Groupist, who was also a student at that time, asserts that Buchman emphasized even then his conviction that the world needed a spiritual revolution. It is quite obvious from the list of his courses as well as his known predilections that he made frequent use of the Bible. One who saw much of him when he was at Penn State and during the early days of the Group says that he was a fundamentalist in his point of view and writes,

> He [Buchman] does not understand the modern approach to the Bible, which he professes to use as a textbook, and he will not read what modern scholars are saying.

A colleague at Hartford complained of his premillennial views. Consequently we can be certain that his Biblical interpretation was fairly literal. But quite clearly all emphases were subordinated to his evangelistic aim.

This same objective was aimed at in his daily contacts with the students at Hartford, as has been noted. For the first year or two he lived in the students' dormitory and ate with the students in their dining hall, sharing their fellowship and their complaints about the quality of the food. He had very little to do with the faculty, but spent much of his time with the students in endeavors at conversion, in which he was only partly successful. It was not long before the student body was divided into two violently opposed groups, those who approved of him and those who disapproved. It was a common occurrence for him to enter a student's room in the evening and remain for a long stay, though the student may have had much work unprepared. It is reported that on more than one occasion he was finally requested to leave. At last, dissension reached such a pitch that it came to the ears of the Trustees, who were much concerned about the possible consequences. As a result, it was decided to request Mr. Buchman to live off the campus, and in his second or third year he removed his residence to a boarding house in the city.

Much the same situation existed among the faculty—though here the opposition to Buchman was more one-sided than with the students. There are stories of violent outbursts of temper in connection with both his critics and his followers.

Apparently he criticized the courses of his colleagues for not being "vital," while they returned the criticism in contempt for his scholarship as well as what they often considered unwise meddling with the religious lives of the students. One story is told of a girl who had "Guidance" to engage passage to Europe with no means of paying for it, another of a young man whose habits were so impeccable that Buchman had to convict him of sin on the grounds of his spending too much money, though he himself had the reputation of being very much of a spendthrift. Furthermore, he had the reputation of being unreliable about his engagements when "Guidance" directed him to neglect them.

But all this is not meant to imply that Dr. Buchman was not on friendly terms with the faculty most of the time. Besides, he had one very powerful supporter on the faculty in the person of President Mackenzie, who, although he did not fully approve of Buchman, was nevertheless large-minded enough to feel that his methods had power and his message value. Apparently he acted as a sort of buffer between Mr. Buchman and some of the faculty, and seems to have deplored the lack of charity on both sides. He wrote appreciatively of Buchman's work several times, of which the following item from his Report to the Trustees of December, 1917, is typical:

> . . . the theological students have had the benefit of the guidance of Mr. Frank Buchman. His work is of a kind scarcely capable of tabulation in statistical description. I think you will be fully satisfied to know that in its aims and methods his work receives the confidence and gratitude of those who are in contact with it or who are watching its results.

With the students his relations were by no means confined to invitations to leave them alone. He had an early morning voluntary prayer group, like the one at Penn State, which certain of the students regularly attended. Besides he was a welcome visitor at many rooms where his good fellowship and sense of humor made him very popular. He was well liked by the service staff, toward whom he was always generous and thoughtful. The janitor at the Seminary Library recalls that on Christmas Eve Mr. Buchman would not only invariably remember Christmas tips but would take the trouble to go to the bank first to have the money changed to gold pieces.

Buchman's reasons for withdrawing from the Seminary are not completely clear, though undoubtedly his feeling that it was his mission to launch a great revival was the main one. He had tested his spiritual power in peoples' lives not only at Penn State and Hartford but in journeys to England and the Far East. Furthermore, he had had some success in interesting wealthy people in work he had been doing, and this doubtless played its part in his receiving "Guidance" to launch a venture and live on faith. It was at this point that he made the visit to Washington referred to at the beginning of this book, when, as he says, his decision to give his whole time to "world changing through life changing" was made. However, it is more than likely that the friction with the faculty at Hartford was an important factor in the decision. There had been some disputes over his expense account about this time, and his withdrawal coincided with the following episode:

About the middle of January, 1922, he made the announcement to his classes of a special course for volunteer students, and by January 17 the faculty had in hand his request to present this. Perhaps because of the President's absence no action was taken for some time, during which interval he was embarrassed by questions of when his course would begin, his annoyance mounting with the delay. On February 14, the faculty (of which he was not a member, since he was only a Lecturer) received a letter from him in which he announced his withdrawal from his position at the end of the academic year. In a letter to him dated February 17, the faculty turned down his request for an extra course with the explanation that the schedule was already crowded and no special courses previously unplanned could be admitted during the year, though there would be no objection to informal meetings. The general opinion of the faculty in this affair was that he was making too much out of a little thing and posing as a martyr. However, it is likely that his decision was at least half made before this crisis. Perhaps the timing of his announcement simply gave him a chance to show a little pique. Certainly the episode alone cannot explain his action. If so, the request of the Trustees of a few years before, that he remove from the dormitory, should have given him much more excuse for withdrawal. Doubtless the affair only clinched the previous half-made decision.

The general impression of his Hartford stay is not a happy one as compared with his career at Penn State. It is hardly alluded to in Group literature. He left bitternesses and divisions on the campus long after he was gone. Even today one can sense the traces of these frictions. The feeling of the faculty still is unfavorable to him and critical towards his evangelistic accomplishments at Hartford. Yet that he did accomplish positive good is borne out by the testimony of ten men and women who came in close contact with Buchman when they were students at Hartford. Though their testimony is by no means unanimous, seven had much good to say of his effect on them, and one of the seven is still an active follower. The chief criticsms of these students suggested distortions of emphasis, especially in the field of sex, while benefits consisted of a clearer moral challenge and a more vivid religious experience.

But again Hartford represented another laboratory step a

little more advanced than that at Penn State. Buchman was growing bolder, and he was learning more about opposition. He left Hartford, apparently not looking back on his career there with great pleasure, but looking forward to a world revival, the methods for which his mind had already pretty well crystallized.

Chapter Five

Buchmanism at Various Colleges

As HAS ALREADY been noted, Mr. Buchman's work at Hartford allowed him long periods for evangelistic work elsewhere. President Mackenzie's report to the Trustees of June, 1918, had the following to say:

> Our Extension Lecturer in Personal Work, Mr. F. N. D. Buchman, was by your vote released for service in China. I have received from various sources letters of the utmost significance. They are written by such men as our graduate, Howard A. Walter, Mr. Sherwood Eddy, and others. They bear unanimous testimony to the extraordinary power of Mr. Buchman's work among the missionaries and native Christians of China. Mr. Eddy's very powerful campaign last spring was very largely due to the work done by Mr. Buchman, who was accompanied through it all by one of our own under-graduate students, Mr. Sherwood S. Day. We are deeply grateful to feel that we have had some part in aggressive missionary work, and hope that when Mr. Buchman returns he will be able to continue among the students of our School the inspiring influence which he exercised upon certain members of our student body during his previous periods of activity in Hosmer Hall.

This contemporary account of Buchman's work makes clear that he was in China during 1918 and that the work was attracting attention. This trip was very important for the Oxford Group movement for three reasons. (1) It was at this time that the conviction forced itself on Buchman that "personal contact of man with man constituted the means of reaching souls." This may have been partly his reaction to the mass methods of "Billy" Sunday with whom he had worked previous to the trip. (2) The formula for conveying his method to others was evolved at this time. The formula was contained in the "five C's" of Confidence, Confession, Conviction, Conversion, and Continuance, produced for the benefit of a traveling companion who wanted a simple statement of his way of obtaining results. (3) The first "Houseparty" was held in China in Kuling, a resort in central China, at the house of a wealthy Chinese lawyer-diplomat. From this time on, his distinctive work was done not as a lieutenant or collaborator but as a leader in his own right. It was at this time also that he acquired two of his most effective disciples. One was the Reverend Sherwood S. ("Sherry") Day, a Yale graduate as well as a Hartford student, mentioned in President Mackenzie's report quoted above. The other was the Reverend Samuel M. Shoemaker, Jr., a graduate of Princeton and at that time engaged in missionary work in China. A very able churchman, he was for twenty years Buchman's first lieutenant in the United States. During most of that time he has been Rector of Calvary Episcopal Church, for a number of years a kind of unofficial headquarters of the Group in this country, where exceedingly vital Christian work has been done, and still continues. These two men became the nucleus for the campaign in the colleges, which waxed and waned during the next six or seven years. It was young men such as these with whom Buchman planned to start his world spiritual revolution.

Friends made in China gave him contacts in Oxford and Cambridge, and subsequent visits abroad, especially that of the summer of 1921, yielded converts in those universities. Perhaps the most important was Loudon Hamilton of Christ

Church, his first convert at Oxford and a leader of the work in England, who came to the United States for a time after his conversion to work with Buchman among the college men of America.

By this time Buchman was becoming self-conscious about the movement and his aim of world revolution. One indication of this is found in the memorandum of Buchman's courses at Hartford for 1921-1922, which refers to the "Recent Movement at Oxford and Cambridge" by which his own activities were almost certainly meant. A Groupist who had been in his classes at Hartford pointed to a passage in one of Buchman's recent speeches, which the student feels epitomizes the message given at that time, long before the Oxford Group got its name.

> The Oxford Group is a Christian revolution, whose concern is vital Christianity. Its aim is a new social order under the dictatorship of the spirit of God making for better human relationships, for unselfish co-operation, for cleaner business, for cleaner politics, for the elimination of political, industrial, and racial antagonisms.
>
> A new spirit is abroad in the world today, a new illumination can come to everyone and bring men and women of every creed and social stratum back to the basic principles of the Christian faith, enhancing all their primary loyalties. The solution of our difficulties must come from such a spirit rising within people. . . .
>
> To bring about this new world order the Oxford Group believes that a world-wide spiritual awakening is the only hope.
>
> Upon a foundation of changed lives permanent reconstruction is assured. Apart from changed lives no civilization can endure.*

---

* F. N. D. Buchman, *Remaking the World* (Los Angeles, Mackinac Press), p. 1. This statement was made at Oxford, July 7, 1934.

Eschewing both the large mass-meeting of the professional evangelists of the day and the highly-organized and publicized college religious conference, Buchman now turned to the quieter method of the religious Houseparty, which he had stumbled across and developed in China. Through his lieutenants and other contacts, he set out to spread his message and influence through the leading Eastern colleges. Young men and women were to be invited not to conferences, revivals, or prayer-meetings but to Houseparties. Here the seeds would be planted that would eventually flower in a world revolution of "changed lives." Probably it was his difficulties with the Hartford faculty that taught him he must be absolutely independent of college control. Hence he gave up his position, held his meetings off college campuses at country inns, and lived on faith. It probably never occurred to him that in freeing himself of college control he was subjecting himself to a much more dangerous control, because more subtle—that of the wealthy people whom he relied on to support him. But they did not interfere with his main purpose, that of "changing" as many lives as possible, in his own way.

Accordingly, "Sherry" Day, in the fall of 1920, joined the staff of Dwight Hall, center of student Christian activities at Yale. "Sam" Shoemaker at this same time became Secretary of the Philadelphia Society at Princeton. At Williams, "Hi" Lyon, President of the Williams Christian Association, and Roger Preston, manager of baseball, both had been touched by Buchman and, according to him, were working for him. John McCook Roots was a convert who was working at Harvard, while a little later F. C. Lawrence and "Cleve" Hicks became associated with the Phillips Brooks House and helped to organize Houseparties. Before he left Hartford Seminary, Mr. Buchman was also becoming interested in the conversion of women, to whom, before this time, he had not paid so much attention. A student at Hartford in 1922 was told that she was the first woman he had worked on, though that may not have been strictly true. However, he did hold several Houseparties for women only, notably one at Farmington, Connecticut, though he soon gave up his principle of "men's work for men and women's work for women," and held several mixed Houseparties. He had some success with girls at Smith, though complaints of a lack of leadership on that campus suggests that success there was limited.

The fate of the movement in the men's colleges was various. At Williams, as has been noted, the head of the Christian Association in 1921-1922 was a "Buchmanite." At the luncheon to meet delegates to the Limitation of Armament Conference at Washington in December, 1921, Buchman apparently impressed a Lieutenant Colonel D. Forster, an English representative. The two visited Williams that winter, where they met, at dinner and afterwards, thirty-five representative undergraduates. Williams men attended several Houseparties that winter and spring, particularly one held at the Wallace lodge at Yonkers, when Mr. Buchman underwrote their expenses. From the end of 1922, there was an interval of inactivity; but in 1924 Buchmanite activities revived with a series of Houseparties. Opinion on the campus ran both pro and con, though it never achieved the violent pitch exhibited at other places. Several members on the faculty were interested though not active. The Dean had been impressed by the effect of the movement on one student who voluntarily came to him to confess cheating in examinations. Consequently he encouraged attendance at Houseparties by means within his power, such as by granting extra "cuts" from classes for this purpose. During the academic year 1924-1925, principally under the leadership of A. Graham Baldwin, President of the Williams Christian Association, there were on-campus meetings of one or more groups. However, by 1926 there was no influential leader left, and this phase of the movement at Williams died away.

For the purpose of the present study, contact was made with eleven Williams men who had attended Group meetings at this time. Of these there were seven who felt that the experience had left with them values of some permanence, and one of these seven still supports the Group. Four reacted negatively to the experience, though none felt that there had been any permanent harm.

At Harvard the course of the movement followed somewhat the same pattern. Buchman's reports to President Mackenzie of 1921-1922 made little or no mention of Harvard, and it was probably not until 1923 or 1924 that the movement became at all active at this University. Even then, in proportion to the total student body, there were probably relatively few students who were active "Buchmanites." Some of the students at the Episcopal Theological Seminary in Cambridge were interested, and undoubtedly some cross-fertilization between the two institutions occurred. For instance, F. C. Lawrence and Cleveland Hicks, both graduates of E. T. S., came to do student work at Harvard, while John Roots on his graduation from Harvard about 1925 entered E. T. S. There were five or six Houseparties for Harvard men in nearby towns between March and June, 1924. On at least one occasion previous to this time, "Sam" Shoemaker addressed a small audience at the Phillips Brooks House on an evangelistic theme, while there was a small meeting of students in a Cambridge apartment in the winter of 1925-26 to meet Mr. Buchman and hear him tell of his recent trip around the world. Because of the presence of F. C. Lawrence and Cleveland Hicks at Harvard for several years following this, the movement continued there longer than at some colleges. Houseparties, usually without Mr. Buchman's presence, still were being organized as late as 1928, and a group of students met regularly at the apartment of Lawrence and Hicks for a morning "Quiet Time," after which breakfast was served to those who attended.

At Yale, as has been seen, Sherwood S. Day, after his tour of the Far East with Buchman, joined the staff of Dwight Hall in 1920, to which he brought the influence of the Buchman movement. It was perhaps in February of 1921 that Buchman was present at an evangelistic campaign at Yale. A student of that time writes that many students disliked his methods of evangelism as too personal, and he believes that Buchman's activities at this campaign undermined his influence at Yale afterward. At any rate the staff of Dwight Hall was divided on the subject, and this division resulted in many sharp disagreements. Day and E. Fay Campbell, another member of the staff, differed on the Buchman issue. As a result, in 1924 they made it clear to the Dwight Hall Advisory Board that they believed the Board should take a definite stand on the Buchman movement. Day wanted all members loyal to Buchman; Campbell could agree to have no one on the staff connected with it. The result was that Day's position was rejected, and Campbell was asked to remain as General Secretary. From the time of Day's leaving Yale in June, 1924, there was little or no direct Buchman influence on the campus.

Though not strictly a project launched by Buchman's followers, nevertheless brief mention should be made of the Student Christian Missions to Fitchburg, Massachusetts, in 1924, and to Waterbury, Connecticut, in 1926. The idea was originally suggested to some Episcopal theological students in 1924 by the Reverend G. A. Studdert Kennedy and Canon Woods, both of England, who visited Cambridge, Massachusetts, and

Boston in that year. Cleveland Hicks, not yet as closely connected with the Oxford Group as he afterwards became, and F. C. Benson Belliss, both theological students at Cambridge, were among the prime organizers of the Fitchburg campaign. About fifty young men and six young women participated in this. There was a camp for three days beforehand at which Dean Charles R. Brown of Yale trained them in street-preaching. Mr. Buchman and "Sam" Shoemaker were also present, though the actual Buchmanites may have been in the minority. Plans were well laid, and the churches of Fitchburg as well as other agencies in the town cooperated. Factory noon hours were utilized for meetings, movie intermissions for talks, and there were even speeches from telegraph poles to the crowds who gathered around. F. C. Lawrence, H. P. Van Dusen, S. S. Day, Lee Vrooman and Edward Perry were among the Buchman supporters who are mentioned as being prominent in that campaign. The Buchmanites were said to be the strongest members of the evangelistic group.

Two years later the experiment was tried again at another factory town, Waterbury, Connecticut, when the Buchmanite influence was a good deal stronger. Samuel Shoemaker was in charge, and among the active leaders who were Buchmanites were Cleveland Hicks of Harvard, C. S. Wishard, a recent graduate of Williams, and A. G. Baldwin and Sewell Emerson of Yale Divinity School. Dean Charles R. Brown and Sherwood Eddy of the Y.M.C.A., as well as local ministers, helped with the preaching. The plan was essentially that followed at Fitchburg. But apparently there was more emphasis at the preliminary camp on preparation by self-purification through prayer, meditation, and mutual confession. The converts made at Waterbury were most of them young, and there was a certain amount of opposition to Buchmanite methods by at least one minister and other people in the town.

It is likely that contemporary accounts in the *Churchman,* an Episcopal weekly, which was not sympathetic, exaggerate the opposition. But the unfavorable publicity of the Princeton episode, to be related in the next chapter, was in the air, and it is significant that with greater Buchman influence there was greater opposition than at Fitchburg.

The Student Christian Mission as such was not repeated after Waterbury, though the Oxford Group campaigns to various cities and countries in the 1930's are very reminiscent of these two missions and doubtless owe much to them. It is interesting to have the reaction of a woman, not now a Groupist, who participated in the Fitchburg mission. She writes, "I think most of us are grateful for the training given us during those years when 'self-consciousness was weakness and Christ consciousness was power'—when we had to think quickly, speak whether we wanted to or not, and be alive to the inner voice of the spirit."

Before we close this chapter and take up the much-disputed Princeton episode, it will be both interesting and instructive to listen to a first hand account of a typical Houseparty of this day. It was written by one who attended a number of them as an active worker with the Group for several years, though he had left the movement by the time the account was written.*

In April, 1924, I was invited by certain college friends to attend a weekend conference with twenty other college stu-

---

* The Reverend A. Graham Baldwin, now Chaplain at Phillips Andover Academy. This account was extracted from Mr. Baldwin's graduation thesis, *A Critical Study of the movement called Buchmanism,* presented at the Yale Divinity School, April 20, 1928, from a copy in possession of Mr. Baldwin, who gave his permission for this use of it.

dents under the leadership of Frank Buchman. Very little was told me about the nature of the gathering because the men who were lining it up knew next to nothing about it themselves. They were officers of the Christian Association of the college which I was attending at that time and were trying more or less desperately to find something in the line of religious experience or thinking that would revitalize an association that was spiritually slumbering. The so-called Buchman houseparty had been suggested to them as one possibility and they had accepted it in a spirit of adventure.

Consequently we found ourselves, about twenty-four of us, met together at the Northfield Hotel one Friday evening in April. The leaders had seen that provision was made for a comfortable and quiet meeting room where there was little danger of our being disturbed. From the moment we arrived to the time we left we were made to feel that our time was our own. We were to feel free to attend all meetings of the group or to attend no meetings. We could come or leave as the spirit moved us.

The first meeting of the group came at about seven-thirty that first evening. The leaders started the ball rolling by introducing themselves by their first names and by giving a very brief autobiography. Important facts were interwoven with insignificant but sometimes interesting details. One man, for instance, had spent four years as a missionary in China and had a blood pressure two points above normal. After the leaders had informally introduced themselves, the rest of the group in turn gave their names, usually adding a few remarks as to who they were, where they came from, what were their main interests in college and in some cases why they had come to this particular "houseparty." These last reasons ranged everywhere from a desire to get a few free cuts from classes to a yearning to find something real in the realm of religious thinking. As the introductions continued there was less and less formality and the spontaneous outbursts of laughter were more and more frequent as touches of humor were introduced. To end that session and to draw a little more closely together the thinking of the group, Frank Buchman told a story from actual life.

It was a story similar to any one of those told in Harold Begbie's book entitled *More Twice-Born Men*. Mr. Buchman told the story well and there were times when the members of the group were moved to hearty laughter; there were other moments when they sat very still and were very thoughtful. It was a story that struck home—one of a man who had been living a defeated life and then something happened within him and a great change took place; where there was defeat there was now victory and a deep-seated assurance that things were somehow to work out.

After the story and an announcement that we would meet, those who wanted to, at seven-fifteen for a "Quiet Time," the group broke up for the night. Some took long walks together. Some went out to try their luck at skiing, for there was still snow on the ground. Some sat alone and seemed lost in thought. Most of us went to bed and slept soundly.

About half the group were at the little meeting room at seven-fifteen the next morning. They came in quietly and waited expectantly. When all who were coming seemed to be there one of the leaders explained in very simple terms what was meant by a "Quiet Time." It was primarily a time of prayer but of the kind of prayer that meant a listening for the voice of God within you rather than talking to God. After all was it not much more important to hear what God wanted you to do than it was to tell him what you needed and what you would like? A few verses from the Bible were read and it was then suggested that we spend several minutes in silence. As I listened my thoughts wandered, sometimes centering themselves around the verses that had been read, at other times wondering if God really spoke to men. He never had to me. A ray of warm sunshine came through the window and its warmth and light caused me to look up. Several of the leaders were writing in tiny notebooks. I discovered later that they were putting down the thoughts that came to them and which seemed important. Certain of these thoughts they included under the head of "Guidance" from God.

After several minutes of this listening, Frank Buchman and others shared with the group some of the thoughts that had come to them during this quiet period and also during the private quiet time that they had held earlier in the morning in their own rooms. One man spoke of having to make restitution to a friend for a wrong he had done him. A few when asked if they had anything to share with the group said that they had guidance that they felt they could not share. Two or three expressed the conviction that we had a great day before us—one in which significant things would happen. It was a prophecy; some of us felt it was true, but wondered what it meant.

The next meeting of the group, at about eleven o'clock in the morning, was what might be called the crucial point of the conference. All barriers were broken down. Led on by the honest and frank confession of one of the leaders who quietly related his own experience to the group, withholding nothing, telling of a one-time struggle and conflict in his life that had led again and again to defeat, discouragement and at times a morbid despair, this healthy and happy-looking individual told also of the experience in which he had come to see that of himself alone he was inadequate, of his finding God and of the new life that it had meant for him. As he talked, the most convincing factor in his story was his own attractiveness and personality. His radiant countenance and shining eyes coupled with his winning smile testified to the truth of what he was saying and many in the group were thinking the same thought as he told his story. The thought was that this man had found something, something real, something that we would go a long way to find.

The group, led by the honesty and sincerity of the man,

followed his example and opened wide the doors that lead to a man's inner life. All pretence and hypocrisy faded. For an hour young men and old men saw themselves and others, not only as they would like to be or have others think they were, but as they really were. It was what Frank Buchman would call a "real fellowship of sinners."

The other meetings were a combination of this same thing plus a more positive note. Man after man came to a point of absolute honesty with self and with others and with such honesty came humility and the crumbling of pride and pretence. There were moments when the crowd was tense. There were occasions of happy laughter and of consequent relief. There were times when men made decisions of tremendous importance in their lives and in some cases such decisions were followed by emotional upheavals, but generally speaking these were temporary and followed rather than preceded the decision. Much was said in the closing sessions of the conference about helps for continuance and the retaining of the experience that had brought with it an inner calm and conviction. Bible reading, prayer, and the sharing of the experience with others, group meetings of those who had now sealed a friendship on an entirely new basis; all these were discussed and planned. From time to time the negative element, and by that I mean the facing of sin and of failure, was re-introduced by some member of the group but generally speaking its day was over and it no longer predominated in the thought of the group. It was truly remarkable how things that are unpleasant disappeared when they had been honestly faced instead of being repressed and shoved back into a dark corner. The house-party closed on the positive note of how we can help others. The members of the group were no longer looking inward except when the occasion demanded but were looking outward.

I have told in some detail my own story of the first "house-party" I attended because I have felt that it would form the best background for further discussion. There have been others I have attended from time to time. Fundamentally they have been very much like this first. I have worked with the leaders of the movement on other occasions and find that the method and principles are usually much the same. The techniques differ of course with the personality and the ability of the particular individual.

Chapter Six

The Princeton Episode

WIDELY REFERRED TO by the opponents of the movement on both sides of the Atlantic was the Princeton episode in which Buchman was asked by President Hibben not to pursue his activities on the Princeton campus, and which culminated in an official investigation of Buchmanite activities there. Consequently, it is important that this affair be set forth in some detail.

As has been mentioned, "Sam" Shoemaker became Secretary of the Philadelphian Society in 1921. He was very able and active, and at the same time deeply convinced of the importance of the movement. It was not long before the Buchman influence permeated the Philadelphian Society, Princeton's Christian Association, whose activities centered in Murray-Dodge Hall. Princeton was often mentioned in enthusiastic accounts of the movement sent by Buchman to President Mackenzie in the winter and spring of 1922. A Houseparty at Yonkers, New York, on February 18 and 19, was mainly for Princeton men; Buchman mentions with evident satisfaction one of Princeton's football stars who he says was converted at that time; and he alludes to giving lectures at Princeton Seminary. Through his endeavors and those of his followers on the campus many lives were changed.

But at the same time there was another side to the picture. As at Harvard and Yale, much opposition was aroused. Talk about Buchmanite methods and sexual confessions went around the campus, while discussions of masturbation and homosexuality in connection with the movement grew frequent. Opposition swelled to the point where certain students, under the leadership of Edward Steese and Neilson Abeel, proposed to launch a new campus publication with the aim of driving Buchanism out of Princeton. The position of these opponents was that Buchmanism surreptitiously practiced unwarranted inquisition into personal lives, was dangerous in its handling of sex, and was stimulating a most unhealthy interest in morbid sexual matters among the student body.

By the next year news of these criticisms came to the ears of President Hibben, who, in an informal meeting of various interested persons, invited Buchman to appear and state his case. Mr. Buchman appears to have done very badly. Instead of meeting the accusations, he told stories of "Bill Pickle" and others of his converts. One of those present who afterward became one of his supporters, but who met him at this meeting for the first time, declares he could make neither head nor tail of his harangue. This investigation, which by mutual understanding was not brought to the public notice, found the Buchman methods "dangerous from medical and psychological viewpoints," according to a letter in the *Daily Princetonian.* It was probably in a subsequent interview that the President asked Mr. Buchman to avoid the subject of sex in his evangelism at Princeton. Buchman replied that he could not, since that was the very thing troubling eighty-five per cent of the Princeton students. To Hibben this appeared to be a slander on Princeton men, though to psychologists it is a commonplace that sexual anxiety and conflict bother the vast majority of normal young men. Consequently he requested Buchman to stay off the campus.

However, the staff of the Philadelphian Society remained

loyal to Buchman's views and methods. Though Shoemaker left to take up parish work, his place was taken by Ray F. Purdy, a former master at Taft School whom Buchman had converted several years before. The opposition to Buchmanism, which had been somewhat assuaged by the ejection of Buchman, again began to rise. It came to a head in 1926 during the Philadelphian Society's annual drive for funds, which happened to coincide with an article on the movement in the news magazine *Time*. This article mentioned Mr. Buchman's preoccupation with sex and also linked him with Princeton. A mass meeting was called by the Society for October 21, 1926, at which an open forum on the subject of "Buchmanism" was held. A large representation from the student body was present, and speakers were heard on both sides of the question. At the end of the meeting a vote indicated that the overwhelming majority of those present disapproved and desired an official investigation. Accordingly, President Hibben appointed a joint committee of trustees, faculty, and students for the purpose of studying and reporting on the activities of the Philadelphian Society.

This Committee was headed by Mr. Edward D. Duffield of the trustees, with Mr. W. Alexander Smith, Executive Secretary of the University, as secretary of the Committee. It contained, among others, Dr. Melancthon C. Jacobus, Dean at Hartford Seminary and a trustee at Princeton; also Dean Christian Gauss of Princeton. The Committee included men both more and less sympathetic to Buchman. A general invitation to the student body to testify before this Committee resulted in the appearance of all prominently concerned in the Philadelphian Society as well as outsiders—thirty-two witnesses in all. The Report, which was published on December 31, 1926, was in general a vindication of the Philadelphian Society and therefore, by implication, of "Buchmanism." The only charge even partially substantiated was that Purdy, the General Secretary, had held a meeting at Murray-Dodge Hall with Mr. Buchman present in violation of President Hibben's wishes. This was technically correct, but while Mr. Buchman had met some students there, the religious activities had taken place off the campus. Two of the students invited had not known they were to meet Buchman. In summary the Committee had this to say:

It has been charged that in carrying it [i.e. personal work] on an aggressive form of personal evangelism has been employed which has been offensive to many; that the privacy of the individual has been invaded; that a confession of guilt with particularity has been set up as a condition of Christian life; that various meetings have been held at which mutual confession of intimate sins has been encouraged; that emphasis has been laid upon securing confession of sexual immorality, and that these methods have alienated a large portion of the undergraduate body from affiliation with and participation in the work of the Society.

We have endeavored in every way to secure any evidence which would tend to substantiate or justify these charges. With the exception of a few cases, which were denied by those implicated, no evidence has been produced before us which substantiates or justifies them. In addition thereto we have the evidence of a considerable *number* of undergraduates who have frankly testified to the great aid and benefit they have received from the General Secretary and his Associates, and have declared that in no instance had they utilized the methods charged against them. . . . The evidence before us convinces us of his [the General Secretary's] sincerity and zeal for the advancement of the work committed to his charge, and while it is true, as he would unquestionably admit, that mistakes have been made by him in the conduct of the affairs of the Society, we believe they are due largely to an excess zeal and an occasional lack of judgment and tact. There has been no evidence before the Committee to show that the mistakes have been serious in character, and they appear to have been due to an over-emphasis upon certain phases of the work. We think it most unfortunate that charges of such a character based upon so little evidence should have been so widely circulated as to interfere with the work the Society is doing.

The Report goes on to suggest greater variety in evangelical approach and more mature leaders for the work.

The publication of this document apparently disappointed the student body, who were looking forward to something more sensational. However, the Report did very little to change the underlying attitude of the students toward the Society. The drive for funds did not achieve its goal. In some minds the prejudice against "Buchmanism extended to all religion. The Cross in the Chapel was taken out and thrown into the bushes. The statuary figure of the Christian Student had to be removed from the campus to protect it from indignity. The Buchmanite members of the Philadelphian Society finally resigned. But even after this, prejudices lingered to such an extent that the religious work of the Philadelphian Society had to be reorganized and its activities on the campus turned over to a society with a different name. It was not until a college generation had passed that the marks of the controversy ceased to trouble college religious activities.

One who is attempting to make a just appraisal of the Princeton episode is at once struck by the disparity between the violent anti-Buchman sentiment on the campus as compared with the seeming lack of concrete evidence to substantiate the sentiment. In our own study we were able to make contact with ten individuals who had intimate experience with the Group at Princeton at this time. Three felt that they had received harm from the experience, and one of these felt that the harm had been lasting. One reported no clearly defined benefit or harm, while six felt the experience beneficial in varying degrees. Only one of the entire group felt the experience had had a bad effect on his moral or ethical *habits,* but five felt that it had adversely affected their *attitude* toward sex.

Of course ten is too small a number from which to generalize with any confidence; nevertheless our findings suggest a somewhat less favorable conclusion with respect to the Group than that contained in the Committee report. In addition to the ten individuals just mentioned others who were students on the Princeton campus at this time report that the student body felt that not all pertinent facts had been brought before the Committee. Certainly it is hard to square what is known about the movement and its methods in those days with the implication of the Committee findings, for the charges that at its meetings the Buchmanites had encouraged the confession of intimate sins including those of sexual immorality was certainly true of meetings attended by certain Princeton students. Doubtless Buchman had tempered some of his methods in the face of the criticism that was rife at that time, and perhaps the Committee's report had special reference to on-campus activities, from which he had largely withdrawn. Yet for several years previous to the investigation it had been the considered policy of Buchman to hold meetings at which the topic of sex was introduced and intimately discussed.

Nevertheless the general tenor of the Committee's report appeals to one as probably closer to the facts than the student opinion. There was no doubt of the high-mindedness and sincerity of the Buchmanite leaders on the campus nor that many students had received much benefit from their ministrations. Also the violence of the student opinion suggests that much of it was unreasonable. Very few among the student body had ever attended a Buchmanite function at all, much less with any sympathetic view to understanding it. The few cases of failure or harm to the personality which did exist, bandied from mouth to mouth, were blown up and magnified out of all proportion to their real importance, the whole situation exhibiting at various times the fever of both the crusade and the hunt.

The truth was that the sexual aspect of the Buchmanite activities was usually handled in a very skillful and appropriate manner, though ever-present were the explosive possibilities that always reside in any situation in our culture in which sex features as the subject matter. It is interesting that several participants, who as students attended Buchmanite meetings in those days and who afterward entered fields of psychology and medicine, have looked back on their experiences and testified that they there encountered a very healthy sample of sex education, particularly when Dr. Buchman was present. Nevertheless, one wonders whether it was the negligence of the Committee, the dissembling of the witnesses, or simply the circumscribed nature of the investigation that led to the failure of the report to acknowledge these aspects of Buchmanism.

In summary of the early phase of Group activities in American colleges, we may note that its influence on many young college men and women at this time was very great. As will be seen from the stories of a number of people, to be set forth in Part III, those who were touched received great moral and ethical benefit of permanent value through an experience that most of them recognize as vitally and fundamentally religious. Many were directed into the service of the church. Dr. H. P. Van Dusen, now President of Union Theological Seminary, in writing of Buchman and his movement in these days, says,

"Of the fifty ablest younger ministers on the Atlantic seaboard today [1934], somewhere near half were directed into their vocation through his influence at that time."* Yet because of the methods of the movement, with its emphasis on small numbers, those touched could hardly be considered more than a leaven in the religious life of relatively few Eastern college campuses. In addition, as the power of the movement increased, along with the prominence given to sexual matters, so did the opposition to it, with resulting prejudice and interference with even the normal expression of college religious life. While Van Dusen overstates the case when he says, "By about 1925 it is probable that not over a half-dozen persons on both sides of the Atlantic would have acknowledged Mr. Buchman as their leader," there is no doubt that at this time the movement was seriously on the decline, and the mass meeting at Princeton in October of 1926 sounded the death-knell of Buchman's revival in the American colleges. From here on the base of operations shifted more definitely to England, and the American collegiate phase of the movement was brought to a close.

---

* From H. P. Van Dusen's two articles on Buchman and his movement in the *Atlantic Monthly* for July and August, 1934. Dr. Van Dusen was associated with the movement for a while in its earliest days. These two articles are written with understanding and objectivity, and are among the most reliable sources of information about the Group available. Subsequent allusions to Van Dusen refer to these articles.

Chapter Seven

Global Operations for a Spiritual Revolution

IN THE FALL of 1926, when things were going badly for the movement in America, its affairs began to prosper in England. Buchman visited Oxford with the result that activity there was stimulated; and soon after, open meetings for witness were held there on Sunday evenings. It was about this time that through his friendship with Queen Marie of Rumania Buchman began to come to the notice of many among the socially prominent who had never heard of him before. It was also about this time that there was established an "inner group" about Buchman made up of a small number of tried and trusted leaders. By 1927 the center of gravity had shifted to England to that extent that the Group was speaking of its "mission to America"; though an account of what was presumably the biggest event of that campaign, namely, the ten-day Houseparty at Minnewaska, New York, indicates that Americans took a large share in the leadership. This account also indicates that the clientele and character of the Houseparties was changing from those of the small student gatherings of a few years before to an older group, though young people were still very prominent. In 1928 an abusive editorial in the Oxford *Isis* threatened to revive the storm of opposition that had swept the movement out of Princeton; but apparently the Group had learned something about meeting opposition, while a certain reaction in favor of the Group was stimulated by the desire to see fair play. Furthermore it had come to lay less emphasis on sex, so that that handle was not so available to its enemies.

At the end of 1927, there was a campaign to Holland, and in the following years a series of very successful campaigns to South Africa. At this time the Group was calling itself "A First Century Christian Fellowship," but it was in South Africa in 1928 that the name "Oxford Group" was adopted. About this time the Group acquired an important supporter in the person of L. W. Grensted, Oriel Professor of the Philosophy of the Christian Religion at Oxford, followed a few years later by an even more important personage, Canon B. H. Streeter of Oxford, the leading Anglican theologian of the day. Another scholar was the celebrated Swiss theologian, Emil Brunner, who became interested around 1932.

From this time on, campaigns and Houseparties became larger and larger, and the horizons of the Group broader. In 1930 a big city revival was held in Edinburgh. An annual "Houseparty" was held each summer at Oxford for a number of years, to which came people from all over the world. In 1930 there were seven hundred "guests," and in 1935 ten thousand! During this time campaigns of greater or lesser magnitude were continually in process both to countries and places visited before and to new ones. In 1932 there was an Oxford Group luncheon for members of Parliament in London, while in 1933 "teams" were sent to the United States and Canada. This same year the Group was to be found active among the League of Nations delegates in Geneva, one of whom, Mr. C. J. Hambro, helped to introduce the Group in Norway, where it aroused much interest among the people and influenced many individuals. Similarly, the Group had a large following in Denmark. Finland, Latvia, France, Switzerland, China, Japan, India, and Persia are other countries mentioned in which the Group during these years worked with varying measures of success.

Among the most controversial of all subjects connected with the Group is that of its relations with Germany in the 1930's. It is difficult to discover the facts since, except on one or two occasions, Dr. Buchman and the Group have had very little to say about Germany and their activities there. This reticence has been unfortunate for the Group, since it has opened the way to wild speculation on the part of individuals and the hostile press. In the account of Buchman's early life we have seen that he had visited Germany. By 1931 a piece of Group literature had appeared there, and it is well known that the Group had ambitions of bringing about friendship between the peoples of France and Germany. In 1936 Buchman gave an interview in which he made the statement of which the following is part:

> I thank heaven for a man like Adolf Hitler, who built a front line of defense against the Anti-Christ of Communism. Think what it would mean to the world if Hitler surrendered to the control of God. Or Mussolini. Or any dictator. Through such a man God could control a nation overnight and solve every last bewildering problem.

In addition, stories, pretty well substantiated, are circulated to the effect that Buchman visited Himmler when in Germany in 1936. There is no reason to doubt that Buchman would have liked to convert either Himmler or Hitler, or that he would prefer Fascism to Communism. But also it is obvious that he would have expected his converts to change their ways. A further indication of rapport between the Oxford Group and the Nazis was the Rudolf Hess incident during the war. Hess flew alone to England presumably to make contact directly with British leaders, landing on the estate of the Duke of Hamilton. Both Hess and Hamilton are said to have been Buchman supporters. However, if there is any truth in this story, Hess failed to receive comfort from any Englishmen whether Buchmanites or otherwise. The newsletter *In Fact,* source of much of this information, charges that many in the so-called Cliveden Set of appeasers of Hitler belonged to the Oxford Group along with Hess and Himmler. Very likely this is true, for it was such people that Buchman wished to convert, though just what is meant by membership *In Fact* does not define. It is most likely that the Nazi leaders saw in the Group a gullible tool in the operation of their policies, which they proceeded to exploit. A secret report published by the Gestapo in 1942 and discovered after the German retreat from France in 1945 indicated that the Nazis considered the Group dangerous to their cause. However, the fact that it was kept secret suggests that there were Groupists within Germany and that the Nazis felt that they still had something to exploit. Furthermore it is obvious that among the thousands of Groupists in other countries there must have been a number of Nazi sympathizers. But there is no evidence that the movement as a whole was so tainted, particularly after the outbreak of war. Groupists played an honorable and even heroic part in the resistance to the Germans in Norway, where the Group was declared dissolved on suspicion of its being a part of the British secret service. Fairmindedness demands that the criticisms of the Group be examined very carefully, for it would seem certain that many of them have their origin in simple dislike and prejudice against it.

In 1936 the Group was again in the United States, where a great gathering of people from all over the world was held in the Berkshires, followed by a large meeting in New York at the Metropolitan Opera House and a country-wide tour.

These meetings were attended by many notables and widely reported in the press.

By 1938 the Group had again changed its name, at least so far as bringing itself to the attention of the public was concerned. Nothing if not alive to the currents of popular thought, it took advantage of the current sentiment in favor of rearmament to launch a drive for "moral rearmament," and from then on spoke of itself as Moral Re-Armament or M.R.A. This does not mean that the name Oxford Group was discarded. In order to obtain a legacy left to "the Oxford Group" it had to incorporate under that name in England. There was a great deal of objection to this, and A. P. Herbert, Member of Parliament from Oxford, tried, though unsuccessfully, to have it denied the right. "Moral Re-Armament" seems to have been used partly as a name, partly a slogan in order to attract more people. Endorsements were sought by prominent people and their names widely publicized. A meeting which filled the Hollywood Bowl, Los Angeles, to overflowing was said to have turned ten thousand people away.

These large-scale gatherings were publicized as "national" or "world" assemblies, and Group literature, with evident satisfaction, particularizes with respect to numbers of people present. For example, we are told that over 25,000 crowded into the British Industries Fair Building at Birmingham in July, 1936, while in 1937, 100,000 people met over the weekend at Utrecht in Holland for an assembly addressed by Dr. Buchman and Dr. J. A. N. Patijn, Foreign Minister of the Netherlands. The "First World Assembly for Moral Re-Armament" was held in 1938 at Interlaken following the inception of Moral Re-Armament at East Ham near London. A mere 2,000 people, delegates from forty countries, attended this meeting; but the "Second World Assembly" was the Hollywood event just alluded to with 30,000 actually present.

But also, shortly after this there appeared small but disturbing indications that some of the most sincere and most clear-sighted Groupists themselves were beginning to question the changed methods and emphases of the Group. The Reverend Samuel M. Shoemaker, Jr., announced in the fall of 1941 that "after careful thought and prayer" he was quitting the Group because of his "increasing misgivings." Other heretofore loyal followers of Buchman did the same, feeling that the Group had forsaken its early Christian emphasis in its utilization of mass methods and was in danger of becoming simply another religious organization.

Not without significance is the fact that by this time the Group had become so huge that the machinery of an organization was forced on it, whether it wished for it or not. Following its incorporation in England, it has also been incorporated in Canada and the United States. Scattered in various parts of the world, as at Caux, London, Los Angeles, and Mackinac Island, Michigan, are various pieces of its real estate with housing facilities for its administrative activities and staff as well as for its guests. Though it still holds to its principle of never literally asking for funds, hints have been getting broader; nevertheless it has supplemented the spontaneous, free donations of the olden days with provisions for regular gifts promised over a period of seven years or longer. A solid foundation of material vested interests is being laid in legacies and investments, and in the literature of the Group, which also brings in a good income. It must be remembered that workers receive no salaries but only subsistence if that is necessary, yet the faithful can see the movement, which has long boasted that it is not an organization, growing daily more institutionalized before their very eyes. Many admirable economies are practiced, and the spontaneity of early days is still apparent; yet the observer is tempted to reflect that every storm is heralded by a cloud no larger than a man's hand.

During the war the Group ran into a number of setbacks, which its critics have made the most of. In 1941 in England the Group applied for military exemption for some of its full-time workers on the grounds that they were lay evangelists. Despite preliminary support in Parliament, this application was overwhelmingly defeated. About this time the Group was engaged in a number of patriotic enterprises to improve national morale under the banner of M.R.A. These enterprises were launched not only in England, but also in Canada and the United States. For instance, in the United States a musical show, *You Can Defend America,* was presented in many cities, while a patriotic pamphlet bearing the same name was published.

In January, 1943, the Group received a great deal of unfavorable publicity in the United States over an application for draft deferment for a number of actors and technicians connected with its dramatic production. Several publications tried to give the impression that these people were draft-dodgers. The Group's case was put in the booklet, *The Fight To Serve,* sponsored by such people as Admiral Byrd, then-Senator Truman, and A. S. Haywood, Vice-President of the C. I. O. Whatever the wisdom of the application or its rejection, there was no evidence that these Groupists, who happened to be aliens, were any more draft-dodgers than countless citizens at home who believed themselves nevertheless in work essential to the war effort. At this time Dr. Buchman was suffering from serious illness, and the combination of circumstances seems to have dealt the Group and M.R.A. a heavy blow.

The war years, like the year of the Princeton episode, marked another low point in the affairs of the Group. Though infinitely richer in supporters than it had been in previous times of trial, nevertheless it seemed to many observers that its fortunes were on a decline that would culminate in its gradual departure from the theater of influence. But one individual at least never lost the conviction that the Oxford Group was God's movement, and that He would not let it fail. This person was Frank Buchman, lying on what was widely supposed to be his deathbed. This phoenix had risen from the ashes of many defeats in his lifetime; pessimism had never been his failing, so that now neither sickness nor hostile critics seemed to him foes that would stop his way.

The next chapter will describe the recovery that took place in the fortunes of the Group and so made manifest the substance of its leader's hopes, with its bid for a hearing in national and world affairs.

Chapter Eight

The Present and the Future

WHILE ACCUSATIONS OF draft-dodging and the illness of Dr. Buchman took the forefront of the stage in news about the Group during the war, things were going on backstage that enabled it to redouble its activities when peace came.

Whatever the designs for a conversion of Nazi Germany may have been, they were dropped like hot potatoes at the outbreak of the war in Europe. Enemies of the Group continued to harp on Buchman's famous interview with the press and his approval of Hitler, but they never brought to light any evidence that the Group wished to traffic with the enemy or was disposed toward anything but bending its efforts toward the winning of the war. From this time on the heroes of Group publicity were apt to be those in uniform, or Groupists who, like Frederick Ramm, Norwegian newspaperman, had risked their lives in the underground in resisting German occupation.

The booklet *You Can Defend America* was sponsored by General Pershing and printed by the hundreds of thousands. It was excess of zeal rather than a lack of patriotism that got the cast of the companion play into difficulties with the draft boards. This was despite the fact that their work had received the approval of President Roosevelt, while prominent industrialists and labor leaders had testified to particular results in morale building that had had a favorable influence on war production. Education was given attention also, and a series of lessons were developed and put into practice in a number of school systems. These lessons have since been published by the Group under the title *The American Heritage*. Effective in presenting patriotic material and pointing out the evils of materialism, the lessons nevertheless bear the marks of propaganda in a certain warping of history into the model of M.R.A. Jefferson, Franklin, and Lincoln would no doubt be surprised to learn that they had practically been made honorary members of a religious organization, namely the Oxford Group; while non-religious Americans doubtless demur at being read off the rolls of patriotic citizens as this material implies.

It was mainly the work in behalf of war production that led the Group to give some attention to the problem of labor relations, though the working classes had been one consideration in launching M.R.A. Primarily a movement for the upper classes, the Group has always been criticized for not giving more attention to social problems and the plight of the working man. The brightest jewels in Buchman's crown had not been the unfortunates and dispossessed. Bill Pickle, the Penn State bootlegger, had worn pretty thin over the years as one of the few examples of how a social outcast could be changed. It was the Queen Maries, the Henry Fords, the Admiral Byrds, Members of Parliament, foreign ministers, and peers of the realm that were featured in the stories told at the meetings and whose names were found most often in the Group literature. Doubtless the criticism had something to do with the turning of Group attention to the bettering of labor relations and the solving of labor problems. At any rate it was during the war that notice began to be drawn to the fact that the Group was beginning to apply the philosophy of change to laboring men, and publicizing the results. "It is my considered opinion that their work in industry has already been worth a sizeable task force to the Navy", said H. Birchard Taylor, Vice-President of the Cramp Shipbuilding Company in Philadelphia, while a mine in Canada reported a 500 per cent decrease in production loss due to absenteeism after a Group team had visited the plant. Tom Gillespie, a labor correspondent from England, had charge of Group campaigns in many cities to smooth relations between employers and employed, and the Group secured endorsements of their work from such leaders as William Green of the A. F. of L. and Philip Murray of the C. I. O.

Not a movement to hide its light under a bushel, the Group was not slow to celebrate in its literature the amazing change of heart that was coming over labor. Up to very recently the pages of the *New World News,* the Group's monthly news organ, was crowded with stories of triumphs of labor reconciliation and accounts of changes of heart on the part of numerous capital- or labor-hating individuals. The technique and the results were almost monotonously the same in every case. The party to a labor altercation is changed by the Group's influence, first starts on himself and his family, and then proceeds to admit to his opponent that he is wrong. The opponent mellows, admits he has been wrong too, and a new era of comradeship opens for all concerned. So glowing are the accounts in the pages of the *News* that one is surprised to pick up his daily newspaper to find strikes still being called when such a successful and simple formula is at hand. At a matter of fact it is even more surprising to find so little said about the Group's success with labor outside of sources inspired in some way by the Group itself or by its supporters.. The truth is that the typical Group gathering is still middle and upper class. Except for an individual here and there, whom one suspects somehow or other of being a showpiece, the laborer and his wife are definitely the exception and not the rule, for the Group is far from that place where it can call itself in any sense a working-class movement. Its influence on labor has been very spotty at best. It has been successful in certain cases. Some laboring people have been reconciled, and there have been cases of converted Communists. One cannot deny the elements of soundness in the Group's formula for labor peace, and there is no fair-minded citizen who will not applaud the Group's attempts to help capital and labor understand one another. But one would have more confidence in its work if a little less horn-blowing were practiced. The methods of modern advertising may be tolerated when a man frankly celebrates his product that he may make money. It is a little harder to accept such practices when the sponsoring agency proclaims perfect honesty as one of its Four Absolutes. Implications by the Group that its methods are sweeping the labor field just are not true.

Something of this same judgment may be applied to the Group's drive for bettered international relations. But here one feels that it can honestly accept a little more credit. Here it is more in its element in the sense that it has had much more experience in dealing with the type of individual likely to be found at international gatherings or running the affairs of state. In addition, it has ideal facilities for international meetings at Mountain House at Caux, Switzerland. This was formerly an exclusive hotel which had run down during the war. It had been bought for the Group by some Swiss friends and put into condition by the Group, partly by means of labor donated by guests. The first World Assembly for Moral Re-Armament after the war was held here in July, 1946. About 2,000 people from twenty to thirty nations attended, including members of several parliaments, the Chief of the Danish General Staff, Catholic and Protestant leaders, industrialists, a few trade unionists, resistance leaders, and some miners from Britain. Since then this has been a yearly event at Caux, with attendance becoming larger every year. In 1948 it was felt to be of sufficient importance for the *New York Times* to have a special reporter on the spot to report proceedings. For the Assembly in 1949, Foreign Minister Schuman of France had been sufficiently interested to have helped with the planning, and was prevented only by the pressure of business, according to Group reports, from delivering a keynote address. Among the attending delegates were five official observers appointed by the American Congress, which appropriated $5,000 for their expenses. This caused considerable criticism in the press and in Congress, but a favorable account of the delegates' impressions of their visit was read into the *Congressional Record*.

Despite all their talk about reconciliation and the positive contribution that they have made to reconciliation among western Europeans, the Group has never made any attempt to understand Communism. It owes this position principally to Buchman himself, whose bias against Communism has been sufficiently evidenced. In view of his cordiality toward Nazism, those people who see little to choose between the two brands of dictatorship distrust the inconsistency of his stand. The frank espousal of atheism by Russia seems to many to make the Communist danger to religion less rather than greater than the more hypocritical and insidious approach that the Nazis had taken, and these people are not impressed by the light this throws on the mental caliber and sympathies of the Group. However this may be, Buchman seems at present to be trying to put himself at the head of a crusade against Communism despite avowals by the Group that it is not a political movement. Yet it would seem to be carping too much to deny credit to the Group for what it has already accomplished since the war in the way of national reconciliation. Even if we cannot trust too greatly the ecstatic plaudits of the Group journalists, and though we do not much notice the effect of the movement in lessened national tensions anywhere outside of Caux, surely if only those concrete evidences of lessening animosities were existent that are documented in the *New World News* there would still be something to say for the Group achievement. "Facing these differences [between France and Germany] honestly has freed me from bitterness," writes a former German fighter pilot. And who can say that a spirit such as this cannot spread, for recent friendly approaches to Germany by France may owe something to Schuman's contacts with the Group. Wisdom as well as charity dictates that the rest of the world at least refrain from obstructionism while the Group is given a chance to show what it can do.

Another slowly growing tendency not obvious to outsiders, but of which some of Buchman's close associates have complained, is a narrowing of the leadership circle and an impatience with criticism. Buchman's sense of humor has never extended to the point where he could take criticism of himself easily, and probably with the coming of age—he is now in his seventies—a certain flexibility that he did show in his younger days has now left him, to the detriment of the movement. At any rate, this development has helped the Group to lose some very able supporters.

Recently there has come rather unexpected backing for the Group from Catholic sources, though the movement is fundamentally Protestant and evangelistic. For example, the Pope's private Chamberlain, Count Castiglione, in 1946 delivered a lecture in Rome in which he praised the Group as a great Christian force and even suggested that it might be the means of a reconciliation of all Christians. Though the Church in the past has on occasions disapproved of Catholics attending

Group functions, these bans seem to be no longer in effect and many Catholics, some of them members of Orders, have taken prominent parts at Group meetings. The motive of anti-Communism undoubtedly has much to do with this support, as suggested by the Count's lecture, printed in the *New World News* for October, 1946. The possible religious implications of this development is one of the most interesting aspects of the Group's activities.

There has always been a certain amount of unpredictability concerning the interests, program, and future of the Group, and speculation on this score is, if anything, more hazardous than most predictions in this unstable world of today. Yet there seems to be a basis for certain generalizations.

Around 1940, Senator Harry Truman had some contact with it, was impressed, and became sufficiently interested to speak at some of its meetings. In recent times, however, his interest has died out. This has been the history of so many persons' connections with the Group that it is a fairly dependable pattern. There always has been an element of the ephemeral and the feverish about the movement, and this may at least partly explain the meteoric ebb and flow in the fortunes of the Group already noted. Consequently it would seem reasonable to expect that we can look forward to a recession of its influence some time in the future. But, like the stock market trader who can only guess what day will record the top of the market, so we shall not know until we can look back with a little prespective just what phase of the Group's cycle is represented by its present status. We can expect most of those who are enthusiastic about it today to have lost much of their enthusiasm a few years from now. Whether it is conscious of this or not, the Group always has relied chiefly on new converts for much of its verve. Yet it is possible, particularly with its high-power publicity, that a wave of good fellowship generated by the Group might sweep over Europe, which, despite its eventual and inevitable subsidence, could leave its marks on future generations.

Another outstanding characteristic of the Group in the past has been its high mobility. Perhaps the previously mentioned genius for the ephemeral has lent a certain urgency to the itch which Buchman and his followers have always had for campaigns in far-away lands. Not only evangelistic campaigns, but even its headquarters have moved from place to place so rapidly as to make anyone but a Groupist dizzy with the effort of keeping up with it. New York, Boston, Washington, London, Oxford, and now Los Angeles, Mackinac Island, and Caux are some of the places which at various times have been designated as World Headquarters of the movement. But now that the Group is acquiring real estate, one wonders how its future mobility will be affected. It would seem logical to expect that the necessity of staying in fewer places would impose a kind of discipline on the Group which will force it to be more of an organization, temper the enthusiasm on which it has fed in the past, and perhaps finally destroy it, unless it grows in ways for which it has had little stomach up to now.

Allusion already has been made to the political biases of the Group and its preference for the political right rather than the political left. It will be shown later how much this is due to certain features of Buchman's personality. He has always disclaimed any interest in politics, and fundamentally this disclaimer is honest for, as we have seen, a world-wide religious revival has always been the aim dearest to his heart. Yet the non-political emphasis which was a fact in the Group of early times is now becoming more and more a pretense. We have seen how the Group was scorched in the flame of Nazi politics before World War II. Today it is happier in its espousal of anti-Communism, for there are many more honest democrats now aware of the danger of the Russian dictatorship, freed as the world is today of the fascist counter-poison. A glance at the pages of the *New World News* will disclose many thinly disguised if not frankly political pages as well as the sanctification of such rightist darlings as Chiang Kai-shek, General MacArthur, and the Greek General Papagos. These emphases help to explain certain liberal thunderings against the Oxford Group as simply an instrument of anti-labor and reactionary interests. Most of these have been as intemperate as Group self-praises, and as ignorant of anything that might be said for the other side. Yet the Group would be well advised to search its conscience with respect to what truth there may be in the accusations and ask itself whether it really wants to be a political rather than a religious movement. To the extent that it is political, this can hardly fail to dilute the force of its religious message, a message that many of its former supporters feel is over-diluted already. As of today, the Group is marching farther and farther down the road to politics and a bid for power.

It would further seem that the Group may be an illustration of the fact that a religious movement diminishes in spiritual force in proportion as it yields to the temptation to reach more and more people. There is also the suggestion of tragedy if the Group should fail not through pursuing its own deepest insights but through forsaking them. There is no doubt that it has its enemies who, in the press and through private gossip, have stooped to distortion of truth and calumny in order to discredit its work. But it has contributed to its own discomfiture. Its recent history is in sharp contrast with the days when Buchman was working in the colleges almost in secret and when he refused to have his name printed in a book about himself because he distrusted publicity. In *Soul Surgery,* the first handbook used by the Group back in the 1920's, we read the following:

> Yet we must begin again and again far down. Christianity began with one. We have forgotten the simple way of the founder of the greatest influence the world has ever seen—how He ran away from cities, how He shirked mobs, how He lagged behind the rest in Samaria to have a quiet talk with *one woman* at a well, how He stole away from crowds and entered into the house of one Syro-Phoenician woman 'and would have no one know it.'

Frank Buchman has taken leave of his own genius to rely on organization and publicity in place of quiet personal contact.

The Group then has presented to the world a mingled picture. That it has been a very powerful religious movement and touched many lives there is no doubt. It has been the most vital religious movement of our day. It has done some harm to individuals, as later chapters in this book will show. It has been supported to a considerable degree by those who represent wealth and reaction; and unwittingly, on occasion, it may have given comfort and help to those who afterward became our enemies. It is becoming increasingly an organization and politically minded. But on the whole it has benefitted many individuals directly and many others indirectly. It has stimulated interest in religion and has been a leaven in the life of the churches. If it is to fail as a movement this failure will come, paradoxically, both from its breadth and its narrowness: from its breadth in its desire to influence many people, with the consequent use of emphases and publicity at variance with its own basic principles; from its narrowness in insisting that only through its own formula of life-changing can God's work be done.

The Oxford Group's aims have been narrow, yet we must remember that from this narrowness has come power as well as defeats, and the fruits of the movement show themselves in myriad ways unexpected by its proponents and unnoticed by its enemies. Some of these ways it will be the function of a later chapter to demonstrate when we set forth the histories of a varied selection of individuals who have come under the influence of the Group. But first, in our next section, there will be a brief study of the founder and the roots of the movement.

PART II

Roots of the Oxford Group

Chapter Nine

What Manner of Man Is Buchman?

IT MAY SEEM strange to include a chapter on the personality of its founder in a section devoted to the origin of the ideas and methods of a movement; but in the case of the Oxford Group it is difficult to separate the two. As this study has been going forward, it has become progressively clearer how important a place the personality of Dr. Buchman has been both in the development of the Group and in its influence. Van Dusen, in the *Atlantic Monthly* articles mentioned above, speaks of his importance to the movement and the stature of the man as follows:

Many who are eager to understand the Oxford Group Movement might think we have drawn too great attention to Mr. Buchman. They are mistaken. It is *his* Movement. . . . There is not one single feature of this Movement by which it may be distinguished from conventional current Christianity which is not derived directly and wholly from the thought and practice of Mr. Buchman. There is not one feature of it to which men bring violent objection which is not part and parcel of the life and conviction of Mr. Buchman. . . .

Quietly, unobtrusively, without the slightest overt dictation and domination, Mr. Buchman continues to be the determinative focus of the Movement—one of the most extraordinary men in a period which may be distinguished in the annals of history as the Begetter of Great Leaders.

Very unimpressive in superficial appearance and manner, Mr. Buchman's ability must be judged by his effect on those who have known him well. Such evidence as has been gathered in the present research has served only to strengthen Van Dusen's estimate. Yet it is not true that the features of the Movement come *wholly* from the thought and practice of Mr. Buchman; for as a matter of fact, almost the direct contrary may be maintained. But in the sense that all these features came to the Movement *through* the mind of Buchman, Van Dusen is perfectly correct. Consequently it will be profitable for us to examine this crucible into which were poured the raw materials of the Oxford Group movement.

As one studies the literature and documents related to Buchman and talks with those who knew him well, there are three salient foci of his personality which obtrude themselves. For convenience and clarity they will be taken as roughly summing up his personality, and they will serve as points of reference in the discussion that follows. It must be understood, however, that they are largely arbitrary, and other schemes might do as well or better. These points are (1) his political ability, by which is meant those traits which would have made him a good politician, organizer, and strategist; (2) his theological simplicity, which includes his lack of emphasis on all things intellectual; and (3) his religious power and intense spiritual gifts. One may think of his personality as a triangle with political ability at one end of the base, theological simplicity at the other, and spirituality at the apex. The secret of Frank Buchman, which includes elements of all three, will be found somewhere within the limits of the triangle. We will discuss him with reference to these three categories and with special attention to those aspects of the categories which help to explain the movement.

* * *

Buchman has great political ability, as the term may be understood broadly. He would have been not only a good politician but also a successful businessman, advertiser, or strategist in any field demanding attention to detail and the handling of people. For example, Stewart, in his *Life of Henry B. Wright,* speaks of Buchman's excellent preparations for special meetings, and also describes him as "a perfect master at connecting men with those who could be of greatest help." This ability to organize detail and manipulate situations, coupled with the intuitive perception of people's needs, which the above quotation also implies, was the foundation of the success of many of his Houseparties.

Another aspect of his political genius is his ambition, Napoleonic in its sweep; for Buchman strives "with no middle flight" to effect the adventurous mission of world revival, which he conceives to be his peculiar vocation on earth. Early in his career, be it remembered, he was accused of ambition by a fellow student and his seeking of a difficult parish as a result is evidence that he himself felt there was truth in the charge. His ambition doubtless is partly expressed by his interest in the wealthy and powerful and must have played its part in his selection of the most socially prominent colleges as the scene for the launching of his movement. It should be noticed also that this emphasis constituted good tactics for the spreading of his influence through the prestige value of the caliber of his converts. But his ambition has also been the source of much criticism and difficulty. The story of his choice of a first parish was one indication of his awareness of his weakness, while his apologies to the trustees of the youth hospice probably was another. Yet the worldwide scope of the Oxford Group owes much to the ambitious visions of its founder.

Mr. Buchman's ambition as well as his interest in manipulating people suggest another factor important to political leaders, and that is the desire for power. Indeed this must be one facet in the make-up of the leader in any field, though it does not always show itself in the crude form of the common politician or the fascist dictator. In Buchman we see it primarily in the form of the desire to convert souls. In less attractive form it shows itself in his impatience with criticism and in personal feuds, as in the case of his relations with colleagues at Hartford.

Another characteristic as important to the spread of Buchman's influence in the twentieth century as the similar tendency of the Apostle Paul to early Christianity in the first, was the wanderlust that seems always to have been one of Buchman's cravings. Beginning with his trip to England and Germany after his graduation from the seminary, he has made countless voyages to the four corners of the globe, mostly on evangelistic enterprises but sometimes merely for rest and enjoyment. Since this propensity showed itself so early in his career, it probably was not simply an expression of his interest in a world revival, for which there is no evidence previous to his Penn State days. This desire to go from place to place also will help to explain why he preferred to go from college to college in his later career rather than settle at one. A passion for travel is not so obviously allied to political ability as some of the other traits we have discussed, but it probably contributed to the worldwide vision which gave his operations such strategic scope, and it aided him in supervising work in widely scattered localities.

To carry out his careful and far-flung plans he is gifted with the capacity for unusual expenditure of energy. In a letter written in 1911 he speaks of having sent "hundreds of postal cards and written any number of letters. Wrote ten today in the interest of the work." This was during the summer when he was supposed to be resting, and the physicians had told him he would wear himself out at the rate he was going. Shoemaker testifies to his tirelessness, even at the end of a busy day, if need arises for his attentions. One root of this energy is plainly his ambition; a more subtle root is his dependence on God and the strength that comes to him from his sense of divine mission. As has already been mentioned, one of his favorite Bible quotations was "I can do all things through Christ which strengtheneth me." This strengthening he regularly receives every morning in his hour of quiet, and to this he ascribes his power. But whatever the source of his energy, there is no doubt of its reality.

His intuitive sense of the shortcomings and needs of others is an important source of his hold over many. Van Dusen says:

> I doubt if there is a psychiatrist in the world whose intuitive sensitiveness to spiritual disease can begin to compare with his acuteness and accuracy. Years of unbroken concentration upon the inmost problems of personal life have furnished him with unique powers of instantaneous and piercing diagnosis.
>
> But to equipment forged by experience is undoubtedly added remarkable inborn aptitude for character discernment. For Mr. Buchman is not only a mystic; he is a psychic as well. Not infrequently, after two sentences of casual conversation with a new acquaintance, he will suggest the presence of secret difficulties which the other has been hiding from his most intimate companions, or even from himself.

Though his intuition is not infallible, and is even due sometimes to private sources of information, yet there are many stories which confirm this estimate of what has become his almost legendary power of soul diagnosis.

His interest in people of wealth and power has already been

mentioned as an expression of his ambition. Brought up as a conservative German Lutheran, Buchman no doubt absorbed the typical attitudes toward authority and position, the more readily in that his own family was relatively inconspicuous. His former pastor, E. P. Pfatteicher, lists as one of Buchman's passions the desire "to hobnob with those in positions of social prestige," and speaks of being shown letters from Andrew Carnegie, which Buchman highly prized. One of the traits most clearly shown in his letters is this almost naïve fascination, in Van Dusen's words, for "the great, the near-great, the would-be-great, or the thought-to-be-great." This trait in his personality is no doubt the root of the Group's well-known interest in the "up-and-outers," an expression early used to express its mission. "Good food and good Christianity go together" is one of his maxims of long standing, while at Hartford he had the reputation among the faculty of having very expensive tastes. Inns selected for Houseparties even in the early days were seldom noted for their inexpensive rates, while today the Group is almost notorious for its lavish methods of travel and living in much of its work. All of this bears the mark of the skillful strategist, if somewhat inconsistent Christian. Wealthy contacts ease the financing of the enterprise, while there is no doubt of the political and strategic soundness of converting first those members of the community to whom others look up. Though doubtless to Buchman himself his activities among the powerful seem to be directed by "Guidance," there would appear to the objective observer to be little doubt of the influence of his own personal predilections.

Closely related to this interest in the great is Buchman's unblushing flair for self-advertisement, though this is curiously mixed with an apparent passion for self-effacement. The flair is apparent in many of his letters. Touches of it are seen in some of his published letters to Henry Wright. His letters to President Mackenzie at Hartford are full of glowing accounts of the success of his work and the impressions that he has made, with scarcely a hint of the failures, disappointment and opposition that he must have experienced, in common with all evangelists. The same characteristics show themselves in his letters to Professor Willard, his superior at Penn State. His report of his zeal in letter writing in the summer of 1911 has already been noted. One of his earliest reports to Willard not only celebrates his own labors at the Northfield conference, but boasts of the figure his delegation had cut at the conference, even to particularizing about the Yale delegate who referred to "our friend from State." Here he shows the instinct of the born journalist or advertiser, and this he used to good effect in his work. The suggestive effect of just the right story of his power to help has often been the force needed to win an opening and effect a conversion. This ability has also been useful in raising money, though Mr. Buchman and the Group have always prided themselves on the fact that they never ask for money. This is possible because the Group members have developed the technique of telling of their work so compellingly that people are glad to give. This special practice of the movement is very characteristic of the leader, who has successfully used it since his Penn State days. One who was intimate with him for many of his early years states that in all that time he never heard Dr. Buchman ask for money. He would simply tell about his work apart from any appeal and the money would be given.

In view of this instinct for publicity it is doubtless no accident that the most influential of the Group's apologists have been journalists or advertising men. Nor has either Buchman or the Group been a stranger to the besetting sin of the journalist in exaggerating and distorting the truth, innocent though they may be of any deliberate intention. Van Dusen tells of a personal experience, when Buchman represented a prominent churchman as being anxious for a visit of the Group to his city. As a matter of fact, the person concerned had desired just the opposite, but in a spirit of toleration had consented to assist in a small way at the opening meeting when he discovered that the Group was coming anyway. This tendency has its implication for the student of the Group movement in that he must always keep himself alert both in reading about and hearing about the Group from its own supporters. Its claims must always be taken with a grain of salt.

But a brief word is due to the opposite tendency noted at the beginning of the last paragraph. Buchman has also his retiring side. At the start of his career he buried himself in an obscure parish. When Begbie wrote about him, he stipulated that no mention was to be made of his own name. People have been to Houseparties and come away with no impression of him at all, so far has he kept himself in the background and allowed his "team" members to monopolize the center of the stage. As has been said before, Buchman was more or less clearly aware of some of his weaknesses; and one has a feeling that his reticence was partly a device for compensating his great passion to be known; probably it was an honest attempt to frustrate what he himself might describe as a temptation to sin. Yet his very zeal for the success of his movement, for "God's work," may have tricked him into concealing this weakness from himself, and the blatant publicity of the Hollywood Bowl days and posings with actresses, may simply have been the expression of a deep-rooted longing for fame given final expression under conditions in which he himself did not recognize it.

A characteristic linked with his intuitive sense for the inwardness of people is his unconventional boldness in confronting them with whatever intimate fault his intuition senses is troubling them. His critics often cite this as an indication of the man's essential impertinence, and there are doubtless times when his accusations have been no more than that. Yet it must be remembered that this quality of boldness has characterized many religious geniuses. Amos, Isaiah, and George Fox readily come to mind. And it was James and John by whose boldness the people "took knowledge of them, that they had been with Jesus." If a man is right in his accusations and thereby accomplishes a useful purpose, he should be forgiven what under normal circumstances would be inexcusable rudeness. That benefits were actually conferred on many Christians through these methods is suggested not only by the vitality of the movement but more concretely by the large proportion of positive responses to the questionnaire circulated for the present research and reported in Part III.

An example of this boldness is the story told by A. J. Russell of the headmistress who asked Buchman what to do with a girl who had stolen. "When did you steal last?" was his reply, which brought admissions of similar delinquency from many in the party. Another is the story told by a former intimate friend of Dr. Buchman, as follows: In his early days Buchman was working with a celebrated evangelist in a college campaign, and the two were anxious to convert a pair of athletes who were being interviewed together. For a half-hour the evangelist had unsuccessfully tried to satisfy the intellectual doubts of the young men; he finally came out to Buchman with the statement that he could get nowhere with them. Buchman went in to them and was immediately assailed with questions on the truth of Christian doctrines. After several minutes listening he suddenly stated, "Your troubles are not intellectual; they are moral. What about the women you were with last night?" Angered, the young men unceremoniously rose to go. "Go if you want," was Buchman's comment, "but you know perfectly well that I am right!" The next day the two young men returned to confess the correctness of his diagnosis and to state they were willing to follow the Christian life.

And Buchman is no respecter of persons, at least in this way. Of this quality Van Dusen says:

> . . . When he feels confidence in his diagnosis he does not hesitate to confront the person with his failing or need, be he peasant or prelate, statesman or archbishop or Pullman porter, chance traveling companion or one of his closest associates. But, his message does not stop with diagnosis. In every instance, with equal assurance he prescribes the needed remedy —however obscure or chronic the spiritual malady, however shackling the other's defeat, however jaunty his self-confident exterior.

These same methods have been appropriated by his followers, and one can easily understand the source of much of the hostility the movement has aroused, particularly when the methods are used by those not so skilled as their leader is reputed to be.

This leads to another characteristic, more difficult to discuss because direct evidence concerning it is hard to get at. This is the interest in sexual confession which Mr. Buchman exhibited during the early days of his work in the colleges. He is sometimes criticized as knowing nothing about the subject, since he is a bachelor. Up to about 1920, his work was predominantly with men. Since then it has included both sexes. There is no explanation for his interest in sex that is not pure speculation. His hostile critics suggest that he derives a certain thrill from listening to confessions of sin. Probably a more obvious explanation, and one which accords better with Dr. Buchman's known zeal for making converts, is that his method of conversion depends on stimulating a conviction of sin. He found that the average college youth was already troubled about auto-erotic practices, so that here was the most direct way to establish conviction. Cure of the trouble with consequent relief was brought about through conversion, which was then made the basis for a wider influence on the personality.

The foregoing components of Dr. Buchman's political genius are oiled by that most useful political asset, a sense of humor. While it seldom goes so far as to enable him to criticize his own deepest motives, it nevertheless is conspicuous at Houseparties in the light touches that make his stories interesting. His ready ability at relieving too heavy-footed testimony by a touch of humor has been an important factor in compelling those at Houseparties to laugh very genuinely and enjoy themselves. Perhaps in this more than any other one characteristic lies the secret of the Group in successfully keeping its moralism from becoming morbid. It was humor applied in just the right places and in just the appropriate doses that kept many of the college Houseparties in the 1920's from unhealthy tension in their emphasis on sex. Perhaps it was the fact that many critics of the Group did not appreciate this feature that led them to condemn the meetings so strongly simply on learning of the substance of the discussions.

* * *

Quite strikingly in contrast to his political shrewdness is Dr. Buchman's extreme theological simplicity, which has been no less important in the development of his movement. It probably goes back to the pietism in which he was reared.

Possibly the clearest statement of the Group's theology—and hence Buchman's own—is that given by a Canadian committee which impartially investigated the Group some years ago. The central assumptions of the Oxford Group are given as six: (1) Men are sinners. (2) Men can be changed. (3) Confession is prerequisite to change. (4) The changed soul has direct access to God. (5) The Age of Miracles has returned (through changed lives, miraculous coincidences, etc.). (6) Those who have been changed must change others.

Much in these assumptions has obviously grown out of or been confirmed by Buchman's own experience, particularly his conversion experience. But even more basic than these assumptions is that suggested by (4)—God as a living, personal reality who communicates as clearly and unmistakably with men as they communicate with each other. Furthermore, to follow these communications from God, this "Guidance," is to "solve every last bewildering problem," whether for the individual life or for nations. The "world-wide spiritual awakening" of which Buchman continually speaks is simply that conversion process by which men become attuned to God and follow His direction. That they should seek "Guidance" and that God will direct them is the epitome of the message which runs monotonously and without change through all his speeches. Expressions such as "God calling," "God-guided," "God-control," "God's guidance," "God's answer," "God has a plan," "God-led," and "God's direction" can be found on nearly every page of the volume of his collected speeches. One finds little intellectual stimulus here. The speeches are too much the same, and give one the feeling that the prophet has neglected the richness of experience and complexity of life.

It is this naïve theology that so many critics find dangerous in a world as complex as that in which we live today.

> . . . What you want are God-guided personalities, which make God-guided nationalities, to make a new world. All other ideas of economic adjustment are too small really to touch the centre of the evil.

Such a statement as the above is typical of his thinking, and while it has its core of religious profundity it is typical in its one-sidedness. Similarly when Buchman "thanks God for a man like Adolf Hitler," he shows little appreciation of the fact that the form of government can make any difference. "They [social problems] could be solved within a God-controlled democracy, or perhaps I should say theocracy, and they could be solved through a God-controlled fascist dictatorship." This theological simplicity also helps to explain what has already been mentioned, his habit of looking up to the rich and powerful. He feels no necessity for questioning either the power or the wealth. All that is necessary is that the individual become "God-guided," and the proper use of the money or the power is thereby guaranteed. The greater its concentration the simpler the job, for the "changing" of one rich man through his power and prestige will have the effect of changing many.

This basic quality of Buchman's thought has also affected many of the practices of the Group, which has been criticized in the past for refusing to account for its funds. This refusal was due partly to the theory that since the Group was not an organization it was not bound by the ordinary obligations of organizations. But doubtless Dr. Buchman felt that where people are guided, ordinary safeguards are unnecessary. At one meeting a former thief was in charge of a cash register "under guidance"!

Again an undervaluation of intelligence is seen in the depreciation of theology and intellectual discussion in Buchman's evangelistic work. "Study men, not books"; "Why talk to men about the Second Coming of Christ when they have never experienced His first coming?" are some of his favorite maxims. The Group formally does not answer criticisms nor discuss theology. It considers changed lives the single and sufficient argument. Neither is it concerned with what a person's beliefs are or even that he have a belief at all. If a person remonstrates that he cannot believe in God, he is simply told to act as if there were one and see what happens. The Group practice of religion is highly pragmatic, and this is an expression of Buchman's own preference for direct methods rather than book-learning and theology.

At Hartford Seminary, Buchman had the reputation of being often unreliable about appointments and duties. This unreliability was an expression of his belief that God frequently intervened through "Guidance" and that His will was to be obeyed rather than man's. Van Dusen tells the story of Mr. Buchman's being "guided" suddenly to leave a campaign he was conducting in order to sail to South America on the same steamer as the Prince of Wales. Such example has not failed of its effect on the members of the movement, and while no doubt the Group tends in general to make people more rather than less conscientious, it has justifiably gained the reputation in some quarters of producing men and women who are quixotic and unreliable.

Another expression of Buchman's intellectual and theological simplicity is his reliance on maxims and slogans. Van Dusen gives a list in his evaluation: "crows are black the world over"; "don't throw eye medicine out of a second-story window"; "every man a force not a field"; "revival which continues in survival"; "interesting sinners make compelling saints"; "hate, confess, forsake, restore"; "woo, win, warn. "J-E-S-U-S, just exactly suits us sinners"; to which might be added the banality, "It's the banana that leaves the bunch that gets skinned" and "Brevity, Sincerity, Hilarity"; "win your argument, lose your man"; "P-R-A-Y, powerful radiograms always yours"; "Confidence, Conviction, Confession, Conversion, Continuance"; "Sin blinds, sin binds." Such slogans, which he repeated again and again at Houseparties, are probably a reasonably good indication of Buchman's intellectual stature. Yet one detects in them the shrewd sense of an advertiser of no mean ability. They suggest the popular evangelist, not the theologian. And if one studies them, he will see how succinctly each one expresses special features of Group philosophy and emphasis.

Partly due to this habit of viewing things so simply is the martyr feeling which one often senses in Buchman. A typical expression of it is the following from an address made in Sweden.

> Criticism is uncomfortable. I know that. It was like a dagger through my heart when I was first attacked. I suffered. I know what it means. But if you are a real revolutionary, you always maintain perspective, no matter what people say about you. No matter how stones come, you go straight ahead. Stones of criticism are so bracing—they just set you up for the day.

In proportion as a person is sure that God is speaking to him clearly and distinctly so will he ascribe criticisms of his work to evil forces and feel himself persecuted. It is his simple view of the relation between God and man that makes Buchman so sure of the "Guidance" that comes to him in his "Quiet Time." This must be an important factor in the sense of persecution that one finds not only in him but among his followers. This is not to imply, however, that a persecution feeling is necessarily unjustified. Furthermore, a feeling of persecution may be a valuable stimulus in a movement through generating a sense of righteousness that releases emotion and makes action easier. This reaction is suggested by the last sentence in Buchman's statement quoted above.

Some may be inclined to look on Buchman's theological simplicity as a weakness. In a sense that is true, for this lack of intellectual emphasis has resulted in many persons failing to find ultimate satisfaction within the Group, as our case histories will show. Furthermore it is a source of danger. Yet on the other hand, it has also been a source of strength in directing attention to action, not thought. It has turned energies to changing people, not to explanations, and has given the movement a drive which might otherwise not have been possible. To the extent that this drive can be traced to Buchman's simple theology, we can say that the success of the movement owes something to it.

* * *

Up to now little has been said about Dr. Buchman to attract the spiritually minded person. Much has been said to justify the views of those who look on him as a simple charlatan and his movement as a successful racket. But what has been said about him would hardly explain his effect on such men as the theologians, B. H. Streeter and Emil Brunner; the philosopher and psychologist, L. W. Grensted of Oxford; the statesman, C. J. Hambro of Norway, or an able clergyman like the Reverend S. M. Shoemaker, Jr. of New York. No final explanations or estimates of Dr. Buchman's religious power can be made here, but at least, through his effect on other people, one can see that it exists; and there are certain bits of evidence to suggest some of its component parts.

Van Dusen very likely puts his finger on the essential key:

> But the central secret of the man's power must be sought . . . in the absolutely unqualified gift of himself to his God and that God's intention for him.
>
> . . . Frank Buchman belongs in that tiny company of the centuries who have known themselves summoned to the surrender of all to the exacting demand of the Divine Will, and who, making the surrender, have pressed on through darkness and light in immovable confidence in the Divine Guardian-

ship of their destiny. A like surrender he requires of every person who would share intimately in the leadership of his work.

This consciousness of his Divine mission is the center at which all his powers focus. It explains the intense sincerity which all who have known Dr. Buchman will concede. It probably is the principal source of the energy he has always manifested. Agnostics may look on this consciousness as an illusion. Whether it is or not cannot be the concern of the present study. But obviously to Buchman himself it is Reality—the central fact of his life. And with it he has obtained results. This sense of Divine mission is nourished by a continuing experience of God's presence in Mr. Buchman's daily "Quiet Time." It is probably a development of the Lutheran piety of his youth awakened to new significance through experiences such as his conversion at Keswick.

In addition there is little doubt that, whatever unconscious self-deceptions he may practice, he consciously holds himself up to as rigid a practice of the moral absolutes as he does his followers. His letters of apology written from Keswick are cases in point, as is also the story of his public admission of having cheated a railroad in China coupled with his subsequent restitution.

One of the inevitable results of his intense and firsthand religious life is a contempt, poorly concealed, for the more conventional type of religion practiced in the churches. It is the old story of the conflict between the Prophet and the Priest that has been going on since the days when Eldad and Medad were commended by Moses for "prophesying in the camp," yet Korah was swallowed up by the earth for questioning authority. This depreciation of Christian forms of expression other than his own seems to have been fully developed by the time of Mr. Buchman's Hartford period, when his attitude was a fruitful source of his friction with the faculty.

He does not officially condemn the churches, nor seek to do other than revive them; nevertheless his attitude is such that this implicit hostility is often found in the movement, to the great concern of many churchmen.

One of the most attractive ways in which Mr. Buchman expresses his religious nature is his interest in the humble and unfortunate. This is usually lost sight of by those who see only his interest in converting the powerful and the rich. It is true that the latter seems to have been his preoccupation of late. It is also true that he has been very rude to lesser personages when his mind has been on his own affairs. But particularly when we go back to his early career, we can see that this interest in people regardless of their station in life, and his considerate kindness, are traits that have shown themselves on many an occasion. We have seen that he gave much time to the down-and-outs in Philadelphia and founded a hospice for boys. His friends cite an old Irish woman whom Buchman brought in off the streets, rehabilitated, and made cook at the hospice; her affection for him many years later was still warm. He was similarly interested in such people at Penn State, among whom he did voluntary work. His two landladies at Hartford worshipped their boarder and often spoke of his piety as well as his devotion to his mother. We have mentioned in an earlier chapter the liking and gratitude of a janitor at Hartford. Distorted though at times it may have been, this spontaneous interest in other people must have played no small part in the development of Mr. Buchman's influence. One senses in most of his former intimates a real affection such as would be impossible if he were merely the man of pure policy his critics sometimes make him out to be.

* * *

In this estimate of Dr. Buchman we have done little more than catalogue his salient characteristics. It will be noticed that his personality is open to several interpretations, which explains why he is a schemer to one man, a naïve child to another, and a saint to still another. But all a person's qualities are transformed by that underlying drive or those ruling passions whose servant he is. As suggested above, Van Dusen has probably put his finger on Buchman's guiding genius when he ascribes his power to his unreserved dedication to what he feels to be God's will. This is strongly conditioned by his will to power over people, his personal ambition, and his genuine love of others. Again we may recall our triangle with political ability and simple theology at two ends of the base and religious power at the apex. Where to put Dr. Buchman's center of gravity within this triangle is a matter for the individual to determine for himself. Our judgment is that it was located pretty close to the top, though it may have gravitated considerably toward the political area during his latter days when so much of his time has been spent in mingling with notables and planning world strategy. Yet ultimately the man is a riddle. At one time he appears as a self-deceived charlatan and simpleton; at another he is seen ministering to some of the world's ablest and keenest-witted leaders. But the complete secret of his ability and power over people we have only started to unravel. Like Iago, if his heart were in our hands, he would still refuse to disclose the manner of man he is; and this not only because he has become distrustful of all outside attempts to study him but partly because he does not really understand himself.

One cannot tell where history will ultimately place Frank Buchman: naïve thinker, shrewd manipulator of men, devoted servant of God. But there is no doubt that thousands in all parts of the world would echo the testimony of an American he influenced in his Penn State days. This man came to State College from a farm, knowing little of the meaning of religious experience. He was converted by Buchman, worked and traveled with him for years, and then left him because he realized that too protracted evangelistic work was interfering with his religious growth. He is now an Anglo-Catholic priest. Asked about the influence of Dr. Buchman in his religious life, he said he owed more to him than to any person, declaring, "I would be a cur if I did not acknowledge the debt I owe Frank Buchman!"

Chapter Ten

Whence Come the Group's Ideas?

In Chapter Nine we have sketched some of Buchman's salient personality traits, for in them we find the origins of many of the methods and emphases of the movement. But unusual genius though he is, Dr. Buchman has not an original mind, and all or nearly all of his ideas can be traced to others. It will be the business of this chapter to set down briefly the sources of the Group's more important beliefs and practices. To trace them is a relatively simple procedure, for, as has been noted, there is practically no influence or emphasis in the movement which has not come there through the mind and personality of the founder, particularly in the early days, which constitute the main focus of this study. Hence it will be sufficient to indicate the formative influences on Mr. Buchman's mind and development, selecting of course those which were involved in the expansion of his movement.

There are in general three important sources of Buchman's thought: first, the conservative Lutheran pietistic influences of his home and the Pennsylvania German people among whom he was brought up; second, the main stream of protestant evangelistic tradition, represented by the Keswick convention in England, which he was attending at the time of his conversion; third, American collegiate evangelism, conveyed through the Y.M.C.A. and various individuals, particularly Professor Henry B. Wright of Yale.

It is hard to find a good description of the Pennsylvania Lutheran pietism which nourished Buchman's youth and early development. Consequently it will be necessary, as well as very interesting, to travel back to the seventeenth century in order to examine briefly some of the ideas of Philip Jacob Spener of Frankfurt-am-Main, founder of German Pietism, and a man with many ideas that are surprisingly similar to Buchman's. These define the main features and presuppositions of a way of life that, handed down through the centuries and clung to by those who preferred to emigrate from their native land rather than give them up, is still alive in the hamlets and small towns of modern Pennsylvania.

Spener's most influential work was a short treatise, the *Pia Desideria,* one of the Pietist classics, which emphasized strongly the following points: (1) The study of the Scriptures. Spener recommended meetings for Bible-reading and spiritual edification, which suggest the Oxford Group Houseparties and the Bible study which has always been one of the Group's chief emphases. (2) The universal priesthood of believers, involving the duty of mutual instruction, inspiration, and reproof. This emphasis resulted in the important place that laymen had in the Pietist movement and finally resulted in the formation of the *Collegia Pietatis* in which lay religion found expression apart from the churches. Here again there is an obvious parallel with the Oxford Group, which in effect really is a lay organization with no official connection with any church. (3) The practical nature of Christianity, which consists not in knowledge but in conduct. This led, as Pietism developed, to the emphasis on the feelings and will at the expense of the intellect, which can be compared to the reactions of many former Groupists, reported in Part III, to the effect that their moral and ethical habits had been stimulated to a much greater degree than their intellectual development. (4)

The evils of religious controversy. Spener was an orthodox Lutheran and made no attack on current theology despite the fact that he differed from many of his contemporaries. He held that personal piety was of infinitely more importance than doctrinal soundness. In the same way Buchman's conservative Lutheran theological beliefs have had little influence on his movement, where the emphasis is on the "changed" life and its continuance in moral perfection, and not on theology. Furthermore, Buchman refuses to utilize argument or discussion of doctrine in pursuing converts, and this has become a general characteristic of Oxford Group methods. (5) The importance of piety as well as learning in candidates for the ministry. This has no strict parallel in Group practice since the Group does not prescribe for ministerial candidates. Nevertheless, if it did, it would doubtless emphasize practical piety. It should be remembered that while at Hartford, Mr. Buchman's lectureship had for its aim just that, and that his differences with the staff derived to a great extent from his depreciation of other courses as not being "vital."

In addition, as Pietism developed, Spener emphasized the doctrine of regeneration, and character transformation through union with Christ, as the all-important religious fact. There was an ascetic reaction to the worldliness of the average Christian, and this has its counterpart in the Group in its implicit disapproval of tobacco, alcohol, and other indulgences, as well as in the self-conscious differentiation of those who have been "changed" from other members of society. Spener also insisted on strict moral perfection as a goal and the importance for the regenerate heart of always striving toward it, which reminds one of the insistence of the Oxford Group on the Four Moral Absolutes. Another minor but interesting parallel between the Group and Pietism might be mentioned before we pass on, namely, that August Hermann

Francke of Halle, Spener's chief disciple, in all his philanthropic work never asked for money but, like Buchman, relied on God to provide.

Enough has been said about Pietism to make clear that the Oxford Group belongs in the Pietistic tradition. There is no way of telling whether Buchman ever read Spener, though he must have come across him in his studies at the Lutheran Seminary. But probably more important than what he read was the religion and presuppositions of those with whom he grew up, modern descendants of the German Pietists who came to America because of religious persecution long before the American revolution. It was doubtless the atmosphere which he breathed, rather than any literal inspiration from Spener, out of which developed what might be called, from one point of view, the Pietist movement of modern times.

We will pass over the influence of German Social Christianity on Mr. Buchman, for, though doubtless important to his personal development, it seems to have had little influence on his movement. Instead, we will next take up the influence of the more traditional Protestant evangelism whose influence, at least at one point, can be detected. Mr. Buchman was always interested in conversion, as his early work at the Lutheran hospice for boys indicates. Also, since he was a wide traveler, even in his early formative years, he can hardly have done otherwise than have mingled with other Protestants who, though of other denominations, had a similar interest. The point at which we know him to have been influenced was at the Keswick convention, which he was attending at the time of his conversion, and while apparently he has nowhere acknowledged any specific debt to the conference for his ideas, an examination of the aims of this convention will yield several points of parallelism to the Oxford Group movement. Again the convention probably supplied a religious climate or atmosphere which surrounded him at the time of his conversion, and it would be strange indeed if some of its features did not become imbedded in him through the experience.

The Keswick convention is a yearly evangelistic conference held at Keswick in the beautiful Lake Country of northern England. It was founded in 1875 by Canon Harford-Battersby of Keswick, after his conversion at the Oxford Conference, and Robert Wilson, to be a "Convention for Promotion of Practical Holiness." It lasted several days each year and had grown by 1908, when Buchman was present, to a conference that attracted many thousands of people, some of whom came from abroad. Participants filled not only Keswick but surrounding towns in much the same fashion as the Oxford Group filled Stockbridge, Massachusetts, and the surrounding Berkshire district in 1936.

Some of the aims of the Oxford Group are immediately suggested by the aims of the Keswick convention, as they are given by a commentator on the convention: (1) Abandonment of sin. (2) Surrender. (3) "Appropriation by faith of God's promise and power for holy living." (4) Mortification of self-life. (5) Transformation of inmost disposition. (6) Separation unto God for service. (7) "Enduement with power and filling with the Holy Spirit."

Other features that suggest the Oxford Group include its non-sectarian character, the daily morning prayer meeting, conversion testimony, the desire of its founders that it not be recognized as a separate organization or group, and the personal work engaged in by the leaders of the convention. Furthermore these leaders were appointed to their work in preliminary meetings after common prayer, and each took his appointment "as being directly of God"; while in one place is told a story of a "call" much like the Group's "Guidance."

This involves an incident where the narrator and Dwight Moody believed that God had sent a letter astray to the purpose that the two might be enabled to work together. There is also the suggestion that confession was sometimes a part of the convention experience.

But the degree to which the Keswick convention influenced the Oxford Group must be pure speculation. Buchman's conversion did not take place at the convention, but nearby, during its progress. Yet its ideas and methods must have been in his mind, and there is no doubt that his plan for a world revival, which soon afterward began to take shape in his mind, owed some of its impetus to the Keswick convention.

A third, and from a specific viewpoint, the most important source of the Group's ideas and practices was the American collegiate evangelism of the early twentieth century, when Buchman was at Penn State and Hartford Seminary, and until 1922, when he severed connections with institutions and pursued his way alone. The particular tide of college religious work whose ebb coincided with the beginning of his own movement, was that which may be said to have begun with the founding of the student Y.M.C.A. in 1858. In this movement, the great American evangelist Dwight L. Moody played an important part, aided by some cross-fertilization with members of the great British universities. Two men whom Moody influenced were destined to leave their mark on Buchman. The first was Henry Drummond of Edinburgh University, whom Buchman probably never saw but knew through his writings; the second was Henry B. Wright of Yale, who was converted by Moody in 1898.

General features of the intercollegiate Y.M.C.A. movement which doubtless affected Buchman's thought and practices were the following, taken from an early list of aims: College

Christian Associations were to promote (1) religious meetings, (2) Bible study, (3) personal evangelism, and (4) inter-association visitation and correspondence. As a college Y.M. C.A. secretary, Buchman at Penn State was expected to and did promote all of these activities. The personal evangelism of the Y.M.C.A. consisted in bringing students in contact with religious leaders who challenged them to "make a decision" or "dedicate their lives to Christ." The "changed life" of the modern Groupist psychologically involves something very similar to, if not identical with, the "dedication of one's life to Jesus Christ" or "decision for Christ" fostered by the evangelism of the Y.M.C.A.

The "inter-association-visitation" of Buchman's day consisted in visits to other campuses by religious leaders, such as Henry Wright's visits to Penn State, sometimes with a group of students, as when he visited in 1915. This religious cross-fertilization between various campuses was the root of the inter-collegiate visitation of the Group movement beginning in 1920 and 1921. Another phase of this aspect of the work was the inter-collegiate student conferences, of which the most famous were those at Northfield, Massachusetts, where student delegates from different colleges came to hear addresses by religious leaders and discuss both general and personal religious problems with one another. Buchman attended and was active at many of these campaigns and conferences, and it is certain that their features played some part in the development of the Oxford Group Houseparty. However, the Houseparty, though really a religious conference, was a distinct modification of the latter. Professor Clarence P. Shedd, of Yale, suggests that the quality of the student work of the Y.M.C.A. suffered from dislocation after 1915, and doubtless the conferences suffered similarly. Buchman's letters in the Hartford Seminary files reflect his dissatisfaction with them. Perhaps this led to his modification of the method in the direction of making the Houseparty more informal, intimate, and, in the early days, small. There were no speakers in the formal sense, which was another departure; which, however, may have also been an adaptation to the fact that Buchman himself is not a compelling speaker. But in general plan the Houseparty owes much to the American student religious campaigns and conferences.

In 1887 Moody brought Professor Henry Drummond from Edinburgh to the second summer student conference at Northfield. Following this, Drummond paid another visit six years later, and made a tour of some of the Eastern colleges. From this time on for a generation his writings were influential in American collegiate Christian circles. Henry Wright was a great admirer of Drummond, and quite likely introduced his writings to his own disciple, Buchman.

The works of Drummond reveal many ideas congenial to Groupist thought, as well as at least one striking identity in language in the title of an address on "The Changed Life." In this Drummond emphasizes the importance of the Will in conversion. In *Natural Law in the Spiritual World,* Drummond's most influential work, he makes clear his belief in the value of conversion. In *The New Evangelism* he states that this evangelism must not be doctrinal and he shows traces of the same scorn of the conventional minister that is common to the Groupists.

But it is the essay "Spiritual Diagnosis," the last in the volume just mentioned, that influenced Buchman the most. In it Drummond says "there is nothing in the philosophy of apologetical religion at all worth reviewing compared with this living power of true lives." He depreciates speeches, conferences, and books, but "if a man would act upon every other man, he can do so best by acting, one at a time, upon those beside him." He cites Christ's habit of shrinking from crowds and teaching in small groups. He says that the function of the evangelist—and here he is almost prophetically describing Buchman—is

to draw souls one by one, to buttonhole them and steal from them the secret of their lives, to talk them clean out of themselves, to read them off like a page of print, to pervade them with your spiritual essence and make them transparent; this is the spiritual science which is so difficult to acquire and so hard to practice.*

It would seem that this must have been the work that set Buchman to the difficult task of acquiring and practicing the spiritual science of "soul surgery." Drummond wanted a science of spirituality so clear in its technique that it could be taught and learned, and it was apparently the definition of such a science that Buchman was trying to inspire when he helped Howard Walter to write the manual *Soul Surgery.* Drummond goes on to say that the duty of the pastor is to get "*over* God towards man," which may have been the genesis in both Wright and Buchman of the idea of "Triangular prayer" where, instead of praying that God help one's neighbor, one prays that God will use him to help the neighbor. Buchman's conviction of the spiritual hunger of people probably was strengthened by such statements in the same essay to the effect that "the amount of spiritual longing in the world . . . is absolutely incredible."

Enough has been said to indicate that the debt of the Oxford Group to Henry Drummond is a very great one.

* * *

---

*Henry Drummond, *The New Evangelism* (Dodd, Mead, 1899), p. 260. Reprinted by permission of Dodd, Mead Company.

Important as was the direct influence on Buchman of Henry Drummond, the indirect influence was probably greater through Drummond's admirer, Henry Wright. As Professor Macintosh of Yale has said, "much of what is . . . peculiarly characteristic of the Movement of which Dr. Buchman is the acknowledged leader and most of what is best in these special characteristics originated far more with Henry Wright than with Frank Buchman."* Consequently, Henry Wright's unique importance in supplying most of the ideas and many of the methods that became part of the Oxford Group movement can best be made clear by treating of him in some detail.

By all accounts Henry Wright (1877-1923) was one of the most effective if not the leading American college evangelist of his time. A man of transparent uprightness of life, spiritual power, and personal charm, he was dedicated to what he saw as God's will. He taught in Yale College in the Classics Department, and later as Professor in the Yale Divinity School, where he gave a course on Personal Evangelism. His death from tuberculosis was the indirect result of years of overtaxing his powers in the service of his Christian faith.

Besides being influenced by Moody and Drummond, Wright was similarly influenced by Robert E. Speer, from whom he got the concept for the Four Moral Absolutes. Likewise he often referred to Horace Bushnell, especially the account of his conversion and Bushnell's idea that God had an exact plan for each man's life.

Among Wright's personal habits and ideas that suggest similarities to the Oxford Group may be mentioned his practice of observing a daily half-hour of quiet, or "morning

---

* From D. C. Macintosh, *Personal Religion* (Scribner's, 1942). Allusions to Macintosh all apply to this volume, which gives considerable space to the Group.

watch," as it was then called. He believed in "two-way prayer," particularly when interceding for another person, by which he meant not only making a request to God for another, but also waiting for God to make use of the intercessor by giving specific directions for helping. This is the basis for the metaphor of the triangle, already mentioned as having perhaps been inspired by Drummond's writing. Wright also believed in "hunches" or "luminous thoughts" as coming from God. Macintosh gives us the following illuminating story about him:

> Upon one . . . occasion he [Wright] accompanied a colleague to the railroad station, and obeyed an impulse to go with him to Hartford. On his return trip, after a short doze, he was awakened by an old pupil of his bending over him. The two rode to New Haven together, the student telling his story to his former teacher. Drink had driven him nearly mad and he needed help desperately. He had been shuttling backward and forward between Hartford and New Haven on the train in order to keep away from the place where he could buy liquor. After their arrival in New Haven Professor Wright wired to a friend in Hartford to meet the boy on his return. Through the steady pull of friendship the young man regained control of himself and developed into a life of sobriety and usefulness. Henry Wright never doubted that he had been led of God to board the train that morning.

However, Wright was not in the habit of accepting all such impulses or "luminous thoughts" as necessarily divine, but, as the Group has done recently, developed for himself certain critical checks on these thoughts. These consisted principally of a test by the Four Moral Absolutes to see whether the impulse were honest, pure, unselfish, and loving.

Finally, as illustrated in the story above, he was in the habit of listening freely to the problems or confessions of young men, who had such confidence in him that they readily brought their troubles to him. Sympathetic as he always was, he never hesitated to challenge these youths to face the real source of their troubles and live lives according to the best that they knew. This reminds one of the similar quality in Buchman, the chief difference being that while Wright seems to have specialized in young men, Buchman eventually extended his attentions to adults as well. In this connection another similarity in method between the two was that neither undertook to prescribe the "will of God" for another person but left that for the private "guidance" of the individual concerned.

It will not here be necessary to go into a detailed demonstration of the indebtedness of the Oxford Group to Henry Wright, since Macintosh has already done this very adequately. It will suffice to list the features which Professor Macintosh considers to be due in whole or in part to the influence of Wright on Dr. Buchman. They are: (1) The planned life. God has a definite and unique plan for every human life and man is under obligation to surrender himself to God's will for him. (2) The "Four Absolutes," honesty, purity, unselfishness, and love, define the substance of God's will and constitute the standards by which the Christian life is to be measured. (3) Confession, with the attendance of deep-going "soul-surgery" when required. In this respect Professor Macintosh states that Henry Wright was more guarded in permitting confession than the Oxford Group in its earlier days. (4) Restitution whenever possible and wise. (5) The "Quiet Time" with emphasis on "two-way prayer" and "Guidance." (6) "Life-changing." But here Macintosh credits the Group with originality in the use of a fresh term to replace the hackneyed expressions "evangelism" and "conversion," and he seems to concede to the Group greater success in the use of techniques than had Henry Wright. (7) Fellowship as a means of realizing the Christian life, or as Henry Wright defined personal evangelism: "the act of influencing a single human will or the corporate will of a group to make that decision which leads to greater fulness of life *through the process of friendship.*"

It was to Henry Wright that Buchman wrote in 1918

> I have just written a friend again today that much of the best in my message is yours. . . . You come nearer than any other man in the sphere of my acquaintance to the one who actually incarnates the principles of Christ.

As has been indicated in a previous chapter, the two men had many contacts during Buchman's days both at Penn State and at Hartford, when he often came from Hartford to attend Wright's classes in Personal Evangelism at Yale. It is strange that in the literature of the Oxford Group there is little or no mention of Henry Wright. As early as 1910 Buchman was using Wright's manual, *The Will of God and a Man's Life Work,* in his classes, and as Macintosh points out, it is pretty clear that the influence was chiefly from Wright to Buchman and not vice versa. In view of the foregoing it might be said that Henry Wright was the spiritual father of the Oxford Group movement.

Thus, in our search for the roots of the Oxford Group, we find Frank Buchman, not standing alone with his God, but drinking from the springs of great traditions, moving from the shadow of better men than he.

PART III

The Group's Effect on People

Chapter Eleven

Foreword to Case Histories

THERE IS NO subject more controversial among those who know anything about the Group than its influence on people. It is the One Thing needed for healthy living, cry Buchman and his Groupist followers; it is the worst thing for the personality that one can possibly imagine and leaves in its train weakened minds, broken lives, and nervous wrecks, assert the opposition. It was in an attempt to reconcile these two violently opposed views that the project was undertaken that is described in this part of the book.

The method was simply to search out people who had come into contact with the Group and ask them about their experience. It was obvious that it would not do to go to the Group and ask for names, for such a list, were it offered, would quite likely be heavily loaded with those names whose testimony would be favorable. In addition many would be likely to be in that emotional state where any objective estimate of the experience would be impossible. Yet it is the people who have had an experience who know the most about it. The problem of how to secure perspective on the experience along with some intimacy with the reality was solved by studying only those people whose first contact with the Group went back a number of years. A questionnaire, a copy of which may be found in the Appendix, was sent to each individual, and from his reply the account of his experience and its effects were summarized with interpretative comments added to the summary. Each case history was altered in non-essential ways in order to obscure the person's identity. It was then sent to the individual to ask whether there were any objections to its use in this form and any comments. A few suggested changes were made, and the results were put in final form, as the reader will find them in the following pages. All names are pseudonyms.

It is important to indicate just how the respondents were selected. The writer and several of his friends who had had contact with the Group in the 1920's got together and listed the names of as many people as they could think of who had attended Group meetings in those days. A few more lists were supplied by interested persons, some more and some less favorably disposed toward the Group. In each case it was emphasized that the investigator wanted cases that illustrated both favorable and unfavorable outcomes. Then twenty or thirty names and addresses were taken at random from the questionnaire in which respondents were asked to list names of those whose contact with the Group went back ten years or longer. In all ninety-two questionnaires were sent out to which there were fifty-five replies. There is no way of knowing how good a cross-section these may be, though it is felt that it is a reasonably good one. Of one fact, however, there is no question. This is that a great variety of experience was represented, certainly enough to explain differences of opinion about the Group.

These accounts were then roughly classified according to the impression given by the individual testimonies. In the next chapter will be grouped those whose experience has been labeled Negative, representing an experience that was intense but usually ephemeral with ultimate results that were more harmful than beneficial. There were eleven cases here. In another chapter will be found five cases where the experience was so poorly defined or slight as to be labeled Neutral. In a third chapter, nine cases have been denominated Partly Positive where the results seemed mostly beneficial though there were harmful indications as well. There were twenty-seven cases where the experience was almost wholly beneficial with harmful results either trivial or lacking entirely. These accounts were labeled Positive, and because of their number were spread over two chapters. Three persons who were still members of the Group filled out the questionnaire and were called Positive Active. Four members of the Group wrote to say that they could not do justice to their experience in the questionnaire so they, of course, could not be included in the study.

The questionnaires were sent out in the early 1940's, while the replies of the respondents allude very largely to the Group of the 1920's. However, some, particularly in the Positive Group, knew the Group in the 1930's and had continued their association with it until after the inauguration of M.R.A. It is interesting not only to read of the varying influence of the Group on different personalities, but to note the estimates of Buchman and the Group by people many of whom knew him and his work very intimately.

Chapter Twelve

The Negative Cases

William Van Riper

William Van Riper attended a large preparatory school and college, after which he entered the Congregational ministry. He is now teaching in an Eastern preparatory school. He came in contact with Dr. Buchman when in college over twenty years ago and reports that his interest in the Group then was warm and appreciative though he was not "changed." He was active for nine years. The income of his family was moderate, and their religious interests were average.

At the time, the experience was felt to be "partly religious," but Van Riper now feels it to have been the expression of obvious needs and enthusiasm. He thinks it benefitted him in helping him to understand people and "one phase of religion." Aside from this he considers his experience to have been very harmful: "practically wrecked my life—marriage and home—career—intellect—cultural interests—point of view." It did not increase his religious certainty, understanding of life, zest for living, or energies, he says in retrospect; though he does not indicate he felt this way during his active interest in the Group. It changed his attitude toward life destructively: "I'm just beginning to recover from it." Regular in his habits of churchgoing before the experience, Van Riper is now "critical and judging." His answers to various questions indicate that the experience affected his moral and ethical habits both beneficially and harmfully. Otherwise, in all other ways it was only harmful, with special emphasis on the harm done to hobbies and interests, capacity to deal with his own problems, and attitude toward sex. In addition it detracted from his intellectual equipment and was completely dominated by emotion. The Group did not introduce him to the idea of conversion, which he had considered before, but only as a possibility. His attitude toward the movement is now "bitter and resentful."

This reaction was not only the most devastating of the experiences reported, but it was one of only two cases of people who had given much of their time and energy to work with the Group whose experiences were not regarded as beneficial in at least considerable proportions. Even here there is the recognition of some positive benefits, which, however, appear lost in the overwhelming consequences of the reaction. Obviously we have here a very complicated situation to explain, with only the main outlines to be perceived. The questionnaire but scratches the surface. In the main the effect has been almost the reverse of that typical of those in the Positive Group. It has been disintegrating, and apparently has decreased motivation and misdirected life energy. The feeling that emotion completely dominated the experience, taken with only average family religious background, suggests a young man swept off his feet and carried away perhaps by Group pressure without the opportunity to formulate adequate intellectual concepts. On the other hand, the fact that the experience lasted for nine years suggests that at one time it had stability, which disintegrated under the impact of some external or internal stress. The Group explanation for this would be, no doubt, insufficient courage to face its challenge, a falling away from the ideals of perfect honesty and love, a neglect of "Guidance." Again, members of his family may have been responsible for a situation which the Group methods and philosophy only complicated. Van Riper's case very likely is one of such complexity that only a psychologist or experienced minister could have unraveled it; certainly the amateurs of the Group could hardly have been qualified to deal with it.

But since it represents only one of its kind in more than fifty cases, we cannot condemn the movement as a whole on this one count alone. Nevertheless it is a case in which there was not only failure but damage which doubtless touched more lives than one, and the respondent himself places the blame on the Group.

Nathaniel Fielding

Nathaniel Fielding came from a well-to-do family, which he reports as only nominally religious. He attended a large university where, at the age of seventeen in 1922, he came in contact with the Group. He was temporarily "changed" and was active in the movement for about six months. He is now a professor of English and poet at his alma mater. He belongs to no church.

He is now very doubtful of the genuineness of his original experiences. They "do not seem to have been entirely 'religious,' though there was not lacking a sense of being under the guidance of what seemed at the time a higher power than oneself." They gave him "in a not very high form . . . some hint of what a real mystic experience might be though I might realize my own incapacity to attain it." But the predominant effect on him was harmful in that it gave him a religious experience without any intellectual content and caused a reaction which led to excess. It increased his sense of the meaning of life only temporarily, for even at the time there was a "feeling, underneath, of something artificial—not natural to myself." Before, his church attendance had been regular, while now he attends hardly at all. The experience was harmful to his moral or ethical habits and his attitude toward sex.

He had not been dissatisfied with his life before the experience and was not looking forward to conversion, the possibility of which was suggested to him by one of the leaders of the Group. He is now "intellectually entirely out of sympathy" though he feels that it does, "in a crude and somewhat dangerous way, rely on values—or rather touch them—that are important and essential."

Fielding's answers suggest a complex nature affected variously by the experience. He might have been classed with the Partly Positive rather than the Negative group were it not that his answers suggest more harm than benefit from his contacts. It is evident that he was young and emotionally carried away by his experience, which he reports as completely dominated by emotion. Apparently his active interest in the Group for six months was not sufficient to stabilize its effects. His intellect required more than the Group could give him, and his reaction to an emotional indulgence led him to excess. Very likely his present lack of interest in the church is partly the result of this reaction.

On the other hand, the experience had its compensations. It gave him some firsthand insight into the nature and value of mysticism. That he was active for as long as six months suggests that the Group did satisfy to some degree his emotional needs, and one may well speculate that the experience contributed something to his poetical talent. In short, we have here a good illustration of both the strength and weakness of the Group. Meeting an emotional need, it nevertheless failed to supply the intellectual balance and refinement necessary to satisfy and keep steady a sensitive mind.

Sidney Thatcher

Sidney Thatcher, at present a master in a preparatory school, came in contact with the Oxford Group in 1922 when he was nineteen, through the college Christian association at the university he was attending. His interest he reports as very warm, and he was somewhat active in the movement during the two months his interest lasted. His parents were Protestant missionaries in moderate circumstances so that his background was strongly religious and had led him to expect conversion. However, he has now become a Roman Catholic.

While he originally felt his experience with the Group to be genuinely religious, he became dissatisfied with "emotional and psychological substitutes for a true faith and rational dogma. Right after the fervor faded I was sunk in rather bitter disillusion, which lingered in me for three or four years—though I now see it as an inevitable phase in my spiritual life." His regular church attendance fell off after the experience until his conversion to Rome. He regards as beneficial the fact that through his experience he made a few friends at college, but it affected adversely studies, moral or ethical habits, and his attitude toward sex. Throughout his answers he makes clear that he now regards the "guidance" of his experience as mechanically directed by the leadership. "I disliked the way he [i.e., Buchman] dwelt on the claim of pure spontaneity—while every meeting ran like melted butter, with the confessions touched off by a trusted disciple and with Buchman always alert to guide any neophyte recipient of individual guidance back to the groove. Yet I fell completely under the spell of one or two firm Buchmanites whom I still admire deeply."

Here is another case where the Group aroused a youth emotionally but was not able to satisfy him intellectually. He reports that at the time he "was going through the common phase of sophomoric agnosticism and general doubts." Probably this, coupled with his religious upbringing and expectation of conversion, led to the experience being for a time emotionally satisfying. But its intellectual thinness paved the way for a disillusioning reaction. Both of these stages Thatcher now looks on as inevitable phases of his spiritual life, which eventually led him to Rome. Aside from reaction to an unsatisfactory religious stage, he does not think that the Group contributed anything constructive to his eventual conversion. One might have expected that his home training could have supplied the intellectual balance which would have preserved positive emotional values, as was the case in other individuals. At any rate it is very likely that his home training had accustomed him to religion in his life as a normal thing. The Oxford Group satisfied this need only on the emotional side so that after a reaction against it he again sought religious satisfaction, but in a form as different as possible from that which had disappointed him. The pat explanation of the Group for backsliders—that they are unwilling to face the challenge of difficult living—does not seem to fit here. Thatcher, in his return to religion, sought out a faith which for him, as a Catholic among Protestants, is no doubt equally challenging and difficult. This would seem to be another clear case of failure of the Group because of its lack of intellectual depth.

Alvin Tucker

Alvin Tucker came in contact with the Oxford Group in 1923 when, at twenty-two, he was invited to a Houseparty for college students. His family's income at the time was moderate, and he describes his religious background as average. He was not deeply involved emotionally and was not active in the movement. He is a teacher and belongs to the Congregational church.

He was never convinced, even at the time, that the experience was genuinely religious. While he might have been classed in the Neutral group, nevertheless there was a temporary emotional involvement to which there came a definite negative reaction, for he says, "I think the experience was an emotional hoax. It evaporated in a week's time, leaving me rather bewildered as to its immediate power over boys, but feeling there was little genuine religious content." The result was to make him "distrust emotional explosions to a greater degree." His church attendance was casual before the experience and remained so afterward. Yet he does concede that it probably caused him to work out his personal problems more seriously.

This is a case where involvement was slight. What experience there was was emotional and not intellectual; hence the net result seems principally to have been that Tucker has become skeptical of the value of emotional religion, which attitude may extend to religion in general.

Thomas Allison

Thomas Allison attended an Eastern college and divinity school. While at the latter he met Dr. Buchman and for a time was warmly interested in the Group though not active in it. This was in 1925 when he was twenty-three. Allison's father was a clergyman in moderate circumstances, and it can be readily understood that his family background was strongly religious. He himself is now a Congregational clergyman.

He thinks that his experience, originally felt to be genuinely religious, can be explained on psychological grounds. He feels that the "guidance" of the Group was often the "rationalization of impulsive desire," while the discipline advocated was commonly an unconscious escape device. He reports the effect of the experience to have been harmful in overemphasizing sex and fostering indifference to social and economic problems. However, it did increase his zest for living, though only temporarily; while at the same time it distracted him from studies and complicated his personal problems. Emotion played a large part in the experience, which added nothing to his intellectual equipment. He had been dissatisfied with his life, but the Group experience provided no basic satisfaction and minimized constructive service. He now looks on the movement as "opportunistic and limited in its appreciation of the social attributes of personal sin and blind to the need for *collective* morality."

There is a suggestion here of the now familiar pattern of a certain amount of emotional satisfaction from the experience without its intellectual counterpart. But here the Group evidently failed primarily because of its lack of a social philosophy. Apparently Allison is concerned with the well-being of people, and in his religion the Social Gospel occupies a prominent place. Since his orientation is largely toward others, he was not satisfied by the Group emphasis on personal morality, individual guidance, and introspective concern with such things as one's sexual life. It is possible that with a broader program of social morality the Group might have enriched Allison's life on a permanent basis. As it was, the main result was definitely negative.

Arthur Manley

Arthur Manley was twenty years old and in his last year at a New England university when, in 1924, he was invited to a Group Houseparty. He was a leader on the campus, being interested both in athletics and religious work. His family was moderately well-to-do and provided him with an average religious background. He now teaches in a small college, where he is much respected. He belongs to no church. His experience he describes as very warm and appreciative over a period of two weeks.

During this period he felt it to be genuinely religious but now sees it simply as a disturbing emotional experience. He feels that there was little benefit in it for him in the conventional sense, while on the other hand it was temporarily harmful due to "a strong counter-reaction and let-down." He says it "(1) caused me to question the validity of all religious experience; (2) left me repelled, disgusted, partly with myself. As consequence broke connections with religious groups, etc." He feels that it left a permanent mark in that it probably made him more aware of himself. Without the experience he might mistakenly have gone into the ministry. As might be expected, it added nothing to his intellectual equipment, for he feels its impact on him to have been completely dominated by emotion. He thinks it probable that he was dissatisfied with his life before the experience, though he has now forgotten. Yet he does emphasize that it was beneficial in a secondary or incidental sense. He says, "It taught me a lot about myself, human nature, varieties of religious experience— which are good and which are bad, at least for me." At present he is completely indifferent to the movement.

Apparently this is a case where the Group experience was definitely negative, except in the broadening and maturing effects which would be the probable results of any deeply moving experience at the same age. There is no evidence that it was even temporarily constructive in producing for him a means of expression, or intellectual activity in harmony with it to balance the emotional factors. Some previous values and aims were nullified. There was stimulated a skepticism which did not lead to any formal religious belief, as was the case with Sidney Thatcher, who looked on the experience as a stage in his progress to Roman Catholicism. That Manley must have achieved some satisfactory philosophy of life is attested by the high regard in which he is held by his colleagues and friends, some of them ministers. While he concedes that the experience may have contributed to this, he mentions no specifically constructive way in which it did. The experience was temporarily disintegrating to his personality, and one gets the impression that at least the immediate influences were almost wholly of a negative nature.

The Negative Cases

Gaylord Brevoort

Gaylord Brevoort was twenty-seven years old and attending college in 1923 when he became interested in the Group. He describes his attitude as "momentarily enthusiastic." He was not active. His family were very well off with average religious interests. He is an Episcopalian and lists his occupation as that of salesman.

At the time of the experience he felt it to be genuinely religious but now feels it to have been more an expression of obvious needs and enthusiasms. Yet he did receive benefit from it through the emphasis on the "quiet time" and meditation, which apparently he still practices, though his attitudes have developed far beyond his naïve first impressions. The harmful part of the experience was his violent emotional reaction. "At the time, it upset me so emotionally that I had to get my minister to straighten me out." Indirectly it may have increased the meaning of life, his zest for living, and his energies, though not his sense of religious certainty. He was not dissatisfied with his life before his contact with the Group and had not been led to expect conversion, which was suggested to him through "emotional impressions and conversions of members of the group with which I attended the houseparty." He has not followed the movement closely enough to have opinions on present policies but thinks that the practices as he knew them ran the danger of taking too literally messages purporting to come from God.

Brevoort might have been listed in the Party Positive group were it not for the fact that the more immediate effects of his experience were negative. He was so emotionally upset that it required the minister to straighten him out. Incidentally we have here an illustration of the value of the Church, whose wise servant exercised a stabilizing effect and preserved positive religious values for the young man. Although the Group undoubtedly played its part in creating this positive side, it would seem that more credit should go to the Church for the ultimate religious adjustment. Besides attending church regularly he also gives evidence of a real personal religion in such statements as "My own belief in God has tended to change from the ideas of the personal God of my childhood to some sort of great unifying supernatural power with which we can become more closely associated through prayer and meditation."

To summarize, we have here the case of a person to whom the Group might have done much harm had not the Church retrieved the experience and stabilized his personality.

Arnold Bullock

Professor Arnold Bullock teaches in a Southern university. He met Dr. Buchman in 1924 at Oxford, where Bullock was a Rhodes Scholar. He describes his interest as at first very warm and appreciative, and he was active in the movement for a year and a half. His family was very well-to-do and supplied him with an average religious background. He is a Presbyterian.

He originally felt the experience genuinely religious and acted on "Guidance" for a while. As a result he "did some very stupid, even dangerous things" and "gave it up as misleading, bad psychology, and bad religion." It was beneficial only "in making me aware of what responsible living really implies, having tried turning over my problems to God to let Him handle them for me." On the other hand, he says it "made me a muckraker—looking for sin and evil in even the most saintly persons. Became morbidly anxious about my own bodily hungers." While it did not increase his sense of religious certainty or the meaning of life, it did temporarily increase his zest for living and energies, but he "became very suspicious of the professional joy, serenity, and sureness of the 'groupers.'" Indirectly his unhappy experience of God-guidance changed his attitude toward life in that it "forced me to trust a heavenly Father, not a mystical nursemaid." His habits of church attendance were regular both before and after the experience. The effect on his college social life was harmful in that he says he became a great nuisance to his friends, while he put his trust in "Guidance" for his studying and failed his examinations. He does regard the effect on his vocational choice as well as that on his moral and ethical habits as beneficial, for he "tried to be honest, sincere, pure, and unselfish"; yet it reduced his capacity to deal with his personal problems in that he tried "putting my troubles off on God or Christ" in a "cheap and artificial" way. Its influence on his attitude toward sex was the "worst emphasis I can imagine." He feels that it actually detracted from his intellectual equipment and that emotion largely dominated the experience. Before his contact with the Group he was "bewildered on vocational choice and what to do about sex." The idea of conversion came to him "through Buchman's suggestion. I felt that I must need it if he said so. I was extremely happy until he pointed out to me how wretched I was!" His present views on the movement are worth quoting at length.

I try to be tolerant, but I am very critical. I know too many persons who have been taken in as I was, and embittered by its false promises. . . . My experience was a whole-hearted, sincere and complete devotion to the movement when it started, to Frank [Buchman] and to his dreams of world conversion. I too had that rather saintly expression I recently saw on a whole flock of groupers who swept through here, and it nauseates me to see how cocksure they are, how intolerant, and how eager they are to share the short cut to God which they feel they have. . . .

I agree with every word of their disarming "moral rearmament" program and know that moral fiber is at the heart of a strong democracy, and I would give anything to be more effective than I am to bring it about. But I seriously doubt their methods as bad psychology and bad education. I am appalled at how little their leaders seem to grow from year to year; the same slogans, same attitudes; and it seems to me they do very little reading.

In Bullock we have presented the picture of a sincere young man who, before his contact with the movement, felt the need of settling on a vocational choice and was worried about sexual hungers. Doubtless at first it seemed made to order. It succeeded in directing him vocationally but only made his sexual problems worse. Besides, his mind demanded a sound intellectual basis for his religion, and the easy substitute the Group offered could not win his respect. Furthermore, his case is a good example of the harm done by the Group through "high pressure" methods. It was insisted that he needed a conversion, though he did not feel so. Also he himself became disagreeable in using similar methods on his friends. His disillusionment must have had some disintegrating effect on his personality, but his fundamental religious instincts were sound, and he did not react against all religion, though it is hard now for him to see anything beneficial in this particular movement for himself. Here the Group had to cope with a young man in college who had definite needs, which were only partly satisfied due to an unsuitable technique and a totally inadequate intellectual program.

H. T. Pitcher

H. T. Pitcher was twenty years of age and attending a large Eastern college in 1922, when through certain associates he first met the Group. His interest was very warm and appreciative, and he was active in the Group for a few months. His family was average in their religious interests and in moderate circumstances. He is an Episcopalian, and his profession is writing.

For a while he felt the experience to be genuinely religious but now considers it to have been the result of "misdirected youthful emotional stimulation." It was in no way beneficial and "harmful in that it absorbed interests and time at a critical period of college life, and warped my judgment." However, he does not feel these or any other effects to have been lasting. He says, "I've been a better churchman since becoming convinced of the charlatanism of Buchmanism." The experience gave a wrong direction to interests and activities in college and took time that should have been given to studies. It created mental confusion with respect to vocational choice. There was no addition to his intellectual equipment, for emotion completely dominated the experience. He had been dissatisfied with his life before his contact with the Group, and his religious training had led him to expect conversion. He now believes "that Buchman is a charlatan and that his followers are dupes; the appeal is to snobbery and to the emotionally confused."

Pitcher's experience was apparently not a profound one; for it is to be noted that there were no very serious or lasting after-effects, as was the case with some of the others in the Negative group. One may venture the opinion that it was simply an emotional spree that temporarily distorted values. From the data given it is hard to see why the movement appealed at all, unless his expectation of conversion led him to believe that the Group offered a road to it. No doubt the vacuity of his own experience contributed much to his present scorn for the movement and its leader.

The Oxford Group

Robert Elser

Robert Elser was a Presbyterian. At twenty years of age, when he was attending an Eastern college in 1925, a fellow student got him interested in the Oxford Group. His interest was very warm, and he describes himself as "on the fringes" of the movement for three or four years. His family was moderately well off and strongly religious, for he reports his father as connected with evangelistic work. He is now a minister and community worker.

As with most others of the Negative group he originally felt the experience to be genuinely religious. Though he does not say so directly, he implies that he is now more critical. Apparently beneficial effects were few. He says that it intensified an already acute sense of guilt, and confession brought no sense of release. Nevertheless, negatively, it "helped me as a religious worker not to make the mistake of prying into people's lives and stirring up emotions without understanding what is involved." And it benefitted his social life in college. "I was rather timid, and the interest of more popular students in me did help me to feel more at home. I was grateful for the interest of these students in me, having a rather strong inferiority complex and sense of being unpopular." On the other hand it reduced his capacity to deal with his own problems and was harmful to his attitude toward sex. Emotion completely dominated the experience and nothing was added to his intellectual equipment. He had been oppressed with a sense of guilt about sex and felt a need for confession before his contact with the movement. Expectation of a conversion was a product of his religious training and also was suggested by the personal interest of two fellow students. He now feels neutral about the movement yet "perhaps a little resentful of the havoc it played with the emotions." His case is interesting in that a later psychoanalysis helped to counteract the harmful effects.* He believes that the movement has been of help to extroverts but in general harmful to introverts, though the feeling of being wanted by a group may partly offset the harm done to the latter class.

This seems to be the case of a very sensitive, religious-minded young man with a sense of guilt about sex who de-

---

* It will be pertinent here to append a quotation from a letter of Mr. Elser in which he comments on the relationship between his Oxford Group experience and his psychoanalysis:

"Before I ever knew the Oxford Group I had some of the same complexes. I had had already a deep sense of guilt related to sex, and always felt the need of confession either to my parents or the person affected—mostly in my imagination. So the Oxford Group did not begin, but rather intensified these particular emotions. Looking at the whole thing now in the light of my subsequent psychoanalysis, I feel that these emotions had comparatively little to do with genuine religious experience. Perhaps I was fortunate in having a very fine analyst, for I do not feel that the analysis had any more bearing on my genuine and normal religious feelings than a doctor who might set my arm after it was broken. For me psychoanalysis did not become the substitute for real religious experience, but rather a specialized branch of medicine which was concerned only with the normal functioning of the mind as part of the body. In other words, far from destroying my religious faith, psychoanalysis helped me to the more genuine and real and not the psychopathic aspects of religious experience. I still believe just as strongly in the doctrine of grace and the place of real 'healthy' conversion experience. In my early years if I had had a normal sense of God's grace, I should not have spent years and years of worry over past sins.

"If my evaluation is nearly correct, then any religious movement at that time might have become not the cause, but rather the vehicle of already distorted emotions going back to early childhood. . . ."

sired fellowship and release. The Group best satisfied his craving for fellowship. His timidity had led him to think that he was unpopular, and the socially successful members of the Group took the trouble to seek him out, which no doubt helped to give him the confidence he needed. But his personality and his problems proved to be more complex than they had realized; consequently instead of confession bringing him the customary release from sexual anxiety, his sense of guilt was increased and his problems multiplied. Neither was sober common sense nor skilled advice available; confusion was worse confounded because the experience was completely dominated by emotion. This is very likely a case which illustrates the danger of the amateurs of the Group meddling with personal problems beyond their understanding. Elser was really helped only when a trained psychologist finally straightened him out.

Aubrey Rowland

Aubrey Rowland is an Episcopalian clergyman who was in his junior year at a small college in 1923, when, at a student conference, he came in contact with the Group. His interest was warm and appreciative at the time, but he was never active in the movement. His family's income at the time was less than $2,000 and his religious background strong.

Originally the experience seemed religious, but now he feels it to have been the expression of obvious needs and enthusiasms. The experience had only indirect beneficial results, chiefly in teaching him to be suspicious of emotionalism in religion. Its primary effect was to make him lose respect for religion. "I had to make a great effort over a number of years to regain a serious attitude toward religion." Rowland's fundamental religious instincts were robust enough to withstand the shock of reaction and even to benefit from the resulting stimulus. "Perhaps without the experience I could not have the religious certainty I have now. I feel that one must have a combination of emotion controlled by reason." His habits of church attendance, irregular before the experience, grew regular afterward through his efforts to regain his religion. In sum total, the experience increased his capacity to deal with his personal problems since he came to recognize the necessity of reason as against emotion. However, it was harmful to his social life in making him suspicious of women, and it gave him a mild disgust toward sexuality in general. Except in the indirect form already noted, it added nothing to his intellectual life, for he feels that emotion completely dominated the experience. He was dissatisfied with his life before his contact with the Group in that timidity and uncertainty were problems. His religious training had led him to expect a conversion, and he had even gone through a "so-called conversion" at a Baptist revival meeting and a reaction against that. He writes that he has little respect for Dr. Buchman, and is suspicious of the movement in its dependence on emotional pressure and its assumption that "sinners will provide luxury and comfort for its followers." Furthermore he feels it substitutes God's effort for individual struggle and offers a dangerous short-cut to spiritual growth. The movement as he knew it allowed no place for the redemptive work of Christ, who seemed less important to the average follower than Buchman himself.

The interpretation of Rowland's experience, so far as effects go, is fairly obvious from the description. A mind that was searching for a reason to feed its faith could hardly be satisfied with the scanty fare offered by the Group. Very likely religious attitudes absorbed in youth kept Rowland from a sweeping and easy reaction against all religion, and he turned to the Church to regain his faith. He does not make it quite so clear as to why he was attracted to the Group in the first place. He had already had one disappointing experience with an emotional brand of religion. Perhaps he was still looking for a genuine conversion, and his uncertainty, combined with Group pressure and a certain emotional need for religious warmth and vitality led him to be carried away unthinkingly. At any rate no benefit was indicated that did not derive from his own individual effort and development.

Chapter Thirteen

The Neutral Cases

L. Thomas Harrison

L. Thomas Harrison was a preparatory school student of sixteen in 1924, when, at his older brother's suggestion, he attended a Group Houseparty. He thought he was "changed" and was active in the Group for two years. His well-to-do family supplied him with a strongly religious background. He is now in industrial work and belongs to no church.

He now feels his experience was wholly subjective, but it was neither very harmful nor beneficial, though he did feel it limited his outlook and types of friends as well as promoting sexual inhibitions. At the time it increased his sense of religious certainty and the meaning of life. Whatever effect it had on his attitude toward life has been completely eclipsed in later development. He has given up church attendance, though through no connection with the Group experience. Except for greater variety of thought and experience, nothing was added to his intellectual equipment. He feels his experience to have been largely emotional. He was not dissatisfied with his life before his contact with the Group, and he was not expecting a religious conversion until this contact. He classes the movement with the Salvation Army and with revivals, where people become intolerant and yet probably do some good. At present he is not sympathetic.

Harrison was obviously young and immature at the time of his experience. Consequently it did not strike deep roots in him; or at any rate it did not block further thought and experience. We can class him in the Neutral group mainly on the score of the seeming superficiality of the experience and the lack of any very decisive after-effects.

Roswell C. Knickerbocker

Roswell C. Knickerbocker met Dr. Buchman when studying at theological school in 1925. He attended one Houseparty primarily as an observer, and describes his interest as academic and yet appreciative also. His family income was moderate and his background strongly religious. He is now a minister in the Reformed Church.

His observations enlarged his religious experience in suggesting new approaches to religion. There were no harmful results, and his sense of religious certainty and his energies were both heightened. He feels there was benefit to his social life and his moral and ethical habits. Intellectually he gained only what one would expect from any new experience. To some extent he had been dissatisfied with his life, but he neither expected a conversion before, nor did the idea come to him through his contact with the Group. He looks on the Group favorably through knowing a number of people who received a new lease on life through their contact, though his own observations in 1925 led him to feel that there was some overemphasis on sex.

In this instance there was little or no emotional involvement. Knickerbocker was almost purely an observer. What benefit there was, was on the same plane as that which a person might receive at the average religious conference. Hence he is to be classed in the Neutral Group.

Henry Clifford

Henry Clifford's case was much like the preceding one of Roswell Knickerbocker. He also came in contact with the

Group while at theological school in 1925 and attended one Houseparty. His interest was academic, and he was not active, though he did for a time participate in a morning prayer group. His family was in moderate circumstances and was strongly religious. He is now a Congregational minister.

His involvement was sufficient for him to feel that the experience was genuinely religious and helpful, "but through fellowship and as a stimulus to the devotional life rather than through any distinctive method." In this way it increased his sense of religious certainty, the meaning of life, his zest for living and energies. But it was one of many influences. It helped to extend his contacts at theological school, helped him to face his personal problems, and led him to discover that his own sexual problems were not unique. The Group added nothing to his intellectual equipment, and emotion played some slight role in his experience. Before his contact, he had had no more than the "chronic sense of need for continuous improvement." His training had led him to expect conversion, to which idea the Group did not introduce him. He is not now particularly interested in the Group since he believes it has no monopoly on religion, though he thinks it may be helpful to some. His impression of the Houseparty he attended was that it was artificial.

The reaction of Clifford suggests that his religious life and background were already sufficiently adequate so that the Group made no distinctive impression on him. It was simply one of many influences, so that his interest was largely that of an observer. What influence there was, however, was beneficial.

Earnest Manning

Earnest Manning was twenty-one and attending college in 1926 when a friend interested him in the Oxford Group. At that time he was active in the college religious society. His attitude was one of curiosity, and his interest never went beyond the academic. His family was very well off and his religious background was average. He is now a retail merchant and attends the Congregational church.

His experience was not in the least religious. He "didn't just know what Frank Buchman was driving at" and could not understand the Group's appeal for others. Consequently it had no influence at all on him, despite the fact that he was dissatisfied with his life at the time. He feels that the movement is completely meaningless but supposes it may do some good for the people who like that sort of thing. He found some of the Group members unreliable in their work with him on the college Christian association.

Manning obviously belongs to the Neutral Group. His case is interesting chiefly as an example of many with religious interests and close contacts with the Group who were nevertheless not at all drawn by it. There is not enough data to explain why. Despite the fact that he regularly attends the Congregational church, he says he is more drawn by the Unitarian viewpoint. This suggests that his religious interests are largely intellectual, to which the Group could hardly be expected to have much appeal.

John Putnam

John Putnam has known the Group movement since 1921, when he was attending a New England university. A close relation was for a long time an active member, and he himself was interested, but mostly he was very critical of it. His family was wealthy. His mother was strongly religious but his father not at all. He is now an Episcopal clergyman.

Since Putnam was never involved in the movement from within, he has nothing to say as to the genuineness of his own experience. He feels that what contact he had was beneficial "only in the sense that it challenged one to look at one's own religious life and attitudes." He believes it would have been harmful to his own spiritual development if he had allowed it to dictate its peculiar course of action. Such contact as he had was almost entirely unemotional. He is now strongly against the movement and believes that Dr. Buchman is an unconscious and self-deceived charlatan. In its early stages he believes it to have been definitely religious, though he thinks the emphasis on public confession to have been decidedly unhealthy. At present he sees it as lacking humility and true Christian charity, totalitarian in spirit, and materialistic. He feels that it was definitely harmful to his relative.

Putnam differs from most other members of the Neutral group in his strong disapproval of the movement. Very likely a good deal of this stems from his close observation of what he considers its harmful influence on his relative. One may also surmise that he himself may have been the object of some of that intolerance of the Group of which he speaks.

Chapter Fourteen

The Partly Positive Cases

William Stuyvesant

William Stuyvesant is a minister and educator who holds a position of important responsibility in the graduate school of a large university. He was twenty-one years old when he came in contact with the Group in its early days, at a large New England college. He describes his interest in the Group as "intimate; both appreciative and critical," and he was active for four or five years. His family religious background was average, and the family well-to-do.

Stuyvesant still feels the experience to have been genuinely religious although he never accepted the Group's interpretation of "guidance." It was beneficial and a challenge to full consecration of life; harmful to some degree in an "unnecessarily radical reordering of character and habits of strength." It increased for him his sense of religious certainty and the meaning of life but not his zest for living and his energies. It gave him a "far deeper appreciation of the significance of religion, and some permanent gifts of religious conviction and experience." While it was harmful to his social life at college, his studies, and his hobbies and interests, it was beneficial to moral or ethical habits and was apparently the decisive factor in his choosing the ministry. The movement added nothing to his intellectual equipment "except in forcing attention to thinking through one's religious faith," and he considers his experience to have been slightly emotional. He was very little dissatisfied with his life before his contact, and his training had led him not to expect conversion, which was partly suggested to him by the Group.

Of his present attitude he says, "It is the source of unmeasured good and of very great harm, both to individuals and to the Christian cause."

The experience of Stuyvesant is ambiguous, but on the whole one feels that constructive elements are dominant, certainly with respect to religion, his chosen calling. It is typical of that of a number of the respondents wherein there was no evident need or desire for religious experience but where the effect was to heighten and canalize religious interests. There is no suggestion that the personality was not well integrated before; Stuyvesant was not unhappy about his life, and one can imagine that without the Group he might very well have gone into other than religious work. The fact that his work is now partly educational bears out this surmise. Throughout there is evident a balance between appreciation and criticism both with respect to his own experience and the work of the Group. He might be cited as an example of the service the Oxford Group has performed for religion in turning towards religious work able men of keen intelligence.

The Reverend Charles Murrow Grace

The Reverend Charles Murrow Grace, an Episcopal clergyman in moderate circumstances, was forty years of age when in 1927 he became active in the Group through a lifelong interest in evangelism. His family religious background had been average. He has now given up his active cooperation with the movement.

He has always felt his experience to have been genuinely religious. "The Group showed me the fundamental *meaning* of Divine Guidance, though I have often been misled on the 'Guidance' for a specific crisis." It was definitely beneficial, chiefly in teaching him to discriminate between conventional and "vital" religion. There were some harmful results due to his "hypersensitiveness and suggestibility at the time." The experience increased his sense of religious certainty, the meaning of life, and his energies, though not his zest for living. He says, "The Group introduced me to an ascetic note in religion that I did not have previously, being somewhat of a religious hedonist, especially their teaching that 'sin is anything that separates you from God or from your brother man or woman.' " While his contact made no difference in his church attendance, he thinks the tendency was to discount the church. It was beneficial to his studies, and while beneficial to his capacity to deal with his personal problems at particular crises, it was not on the whole conducive to his complete integration. He mentions nothing which it added to his intellectual equipment and believes the experience to have been moderately emotional. He had been dissatisfied with his life before his contact and had looked forward to a conversion, which he experienced through the Group. However, while this solved some conflicts, it created others, which made the experience incomplete and unsatisfactory. He believes the movement ideal for (a) young people of fifteen to thirty; (b) people with no previous religious experience; (c) people facing moral crises; but of doubtful value to those who find a real spiritual home in the Christian Church.

Grace's nature is doubtless much too complex for his answers to the questionnaire to give more than the very general outlines of his experience with the Group. The roots of his interest in the movement are clearly the same as his interest in evangelism in general, and these may have been partly the hope for a solution to the conflicts mentioned above. To him it was "superlative evangelism." But the failure of conversion to rid him of conflicts suggests subtleties of mental make-up with which the Group's simple formulas could not cope. On the other hand the experience brought to him a new and invigorating conception of his religious faith. Consequently, this lack of a clear-cut picture leads us to class him with the Partly Positive rather than the Positive group.

FRANCIS MURRAY

Francis Murray was attending a university in 1923 when through the influence of some friends he attended several Houseparties. His interest was very warm. On the campus he was active in many things including religion and athletics. His father is a prominent educator, whose income at the time was very ample. The family life was strongly religious, and Murray is now a Congregational minister.

He felt the experience to be genuinely religious at the time. He still feels so in the main, yet now he feels that a good deal of it was the result of unwise and artificial pressure as well as a too-simple explanation of divine guidance. It is difficult for him to analyze the experience clearly. He says, "No amount of perspective can remove the mixed sensations of great depth and great shame and confusion which prevent a clear analysis." But on the whole he feels the experience was beneficial in "forcing" his growth spiritually and giving him courage to speak of his religious life—"a thing I rarely do now except by indirection." He continues the practice of the morning watch or "quiet time," to which the Group introduced him. On the other hand, its distortion of sex values tended to interfere with the "normal preliminaries of marriage," though this he does not believe left too deep a scar. The experience increased the meaning of life, possibly his sense of religious certainty and zest for living, though not his energies. It was somewhat beneficial to his social life in college in that it "gave a specious shot in the arm to various friendships," and "it may have added one increment of pressure in the set of influences that made me feel the ministry was my life work." It was somewhat beneficial to his moral and ethical habits, and to his capacity to deal with his own personal problems. For him the experience was largely emotional and added nothing intellectually. He had not been particularly dissatisfied with his life, but his religious training had led him to look forward to conversion to some degree. However, he believes it put too much stress on "changing" and too little on religious development, and carried "guidance" to an impossible extreme, though it did "have the value of simplifying the major concepts of religion to the point where any moron could understand them." He also deplores the Group's "all-or-nothing attitude in the physical contact of boys and girls."

That this case belongs in the partly positive group is suggested by the difficulty Murray has in analyzing it. It is evident that the complete story is much too complex for a brief questionnaire, and it is hazardous even to guess at the main outlines. But it seems probable that he was attracted to the Group through his natural interest in things religious, and very likely found through it an outlet for the expression of his pent-up internal religious life. This would explain its bringing to him an increase in the sense of the meaning of life. On the other hand, the Group could not satisfy his intelligence and therefore had no permanent hold upon him.

CHARLES JONES

Charles Jones was in his last year of college in 1926 when he attended a Houseparty. His interest was "appreciative," and he was somewhat active in the movement for a few months. His family was in moderate circumstances and was strongly religious. He is now a Methodist minister.

The experience was never completely satisfying to him, and

yet it seemed to him a religious experience which at least partially met very fundamental needs. It was beneficial in its call for "surrender" and commitment, and was one factor in leading him into the ministry. He believes its subjective emphasis may have been harmful to him, but on the other hand it heightened his sense of the meaning of life. The experience was for him only slightly emotional, but it added nothing to his intellectual life. Before his contact he was "dissatisfied with my lack of a clear purpose in life and the gap between my life and Christian ideals." The idea of conversion was nothing new to him. His comments on the Group well express a common criticism of many socially minded people and hence are worth quoting at some length.

On the whole . . . what they [i.e, members of the Group] have done for individuals I have known to be good.

My criticism of the movement . . . is its relation to what they do for the individual as a member of society. I refer to their theory that if you convert the individual you have done all that is necessary to bring the Kingdom of God. Their strategy of seeking to convert key men in politics . . . and industry without helping those men to see the social consequences of their use of economic power, leaving them blind to those consequences, is to me a socially vicious strategy. Vicious because without changing anti-social attitudes . . . the Oxford Group tends to sanctify them—which makes the necessary changes more difficult still.

The theory that you can work from the top of society down as a sort of short-cut to the good society is a dangerous one.

In Jones we have the picture of a sincere and high-minded young man who was bothered by his lack of clear purpose in life and the gap between his Christian profession and its practice. To him the Group offered in clear-cut form a challenge to his best nature and in this way partly solved the conflict within him. It is quite likely that this then helped clear the way for his decision "to devote my life to some form of service." He says, "The experience of 'guidance' was never very real to me," which, along with other aspects of his testimony, suggests that his personality is oriented toward social rather than mystical religion. Consequently, though Jones is not blind to the necessity for personal religious experience, the Group's lack of a thorough social philosophy and all-but-exclusive emphasis on the mystical experience of "Guidance" kept it from giving him complete satisfaction.

George Elwood

In 1923 George Elwood became interested in the Group when he was an undergraduate in college. He was "changed" and was active with the movement for five years. His family was well-to-do, and his background was strongly religious. He is now an Episcopalian clergyman.

He still feels that the experience was genuinely religious, although now he would make qualifications that would not have occurred to him at the time. On the whole he feels its influence to have been beneficial chiefly as the incentive which led him to his life work. But it was harmful in making him intolerant and raising religious issues which were not fundamental. In addition, his break with it caused a period of uncertainty and disillusionment. He feels his experience increased his sense of religious certainty and the meaning of life on the whole, however. The effect on his moral and ethical habits was beneficial, but, on his attitude toward sex, harmful. It had both beneficial and harmful effects on his social life in college. The experience was largely emotional, and he mentions nothing it added to his intellectual equipment. He had not expected a religious conversion, which, however, did come to him through his decision to go into the ministry. He now regards the Group with sympathetic interest but with the general feeling that its influence has ceased to be important.

Elwood's experience appears to center on the fact that the Group was the means of his entering the ministry, though his family background no doubt helped to prepare the way. But that it was not a completely healthy experience for him is indicated by the intolerance it caused, his period of readjustment after his break with the Group, and his estimate of the distortion of his sexual attitudes. Chiefly, however, Elwood illustrates the power of the Group to turn young men toward the ministry.

S. Carr Reeves

S. Carr Reeves was a theological student in 1920 when he was introduced to the Oxford Group by Dr. Buchman himself. His interest he describes as "warmly appreciative," and he was active in the movement for the period of a year. His family was in moderate circumstances and strongly religious. He is now a minister.

At the time he felt the experience to be religious, but now looks on the guidance he received as partly from God and partly the result of his own desires as well as the suggestions of others. The experience was beneficial in that it "helped me realize the need for facing one's sins and dedicating one's whole life to Christ and His way, and helping others to live the Christian life, the value of daily Bible reading and personal prayer." It was harmful to him "in its over-emphasis of the emotional side of religion, in the unrestrained public confession of sins, in the reliance on divine guidance to determine all activity, and in its often unintelligent efforts to convert everyone." It helped to increase his sense of religious certainty, the meaning of life, and zest for living. In general it helped to make religion more vivid and personal. It was beneficial to him in his dealing with others, strengthened his vocational choice, and helped his moral and ethical habits. It was harmful in discouraging wide intellectual studies. It increased his capacity to deal with his personal problems in some instances and hindered it in others, while it was harmful in putting too much emphasis on sex. Except perhaps for the more personal application of Bible teachings to life, the experience added nothing to his intellectual equipment, being felt by him to be largely emotional. He was not especially dissatisfied with his life before his contact, and was not expecting conversion, the need for which was suggested to him by Dr. Buchman. He believes the Group does some good to those it reaches in making religion more real, but fails to create an intelligent understanding of social problems and religion's relation to them, and associates too much with the well-to-do.

Since the positive aspects of Reeves' testimony seem so much more convincing than the negative, he might have been classed with the Positive group. Yet his feeling seems to be that the harm was not inconsiderable, so that he is more properly classed as Partly Positive. It is not clear just why he was attracted to the movement if other than by his general interest in anything that promised to make his religious life more vital. This it evidently accomplished, but along with it the Group fostered certain distortions and fallacies, which, however, were apparently outgrown. The more positive features of the experience seem to have been permanently absorbed.

Susan Robertson

Susan Ellen Robertson is a teacher of English in a New Jersey high school who came in contact with the Group in 1936 when she was thirty-two. Being interested in religious subjects she had read about the Group and also known of it through friends. Her interest was "warm and appreciative," and for several years she was a convinced and sincere member. She and her family were in moderate circumstances. Her father is a strong church member, while her mother seldom attends church. Miss Robertson is a Congregationalist.

For a time she felt the Group might satisfy her "longing for a vital and transforming religious experience," but she withdrew as a result of a very unfortunate, "over-zealous attempt to follow 'guidance.' " The experience was beneficial in that it helped her to realize "that religion is not fundamentally a matter of accepting certain stated beliefs or performing certain outward acts but is rather a man's relationship to God and his relation to other people." She concurs in the Group emphasis on the need for surrender to God and on good will as the basis for relationships between people. Never before or since has she experienced "the warmth of fellowship which seemed to be usual in Group meetings and houseparties. People seemed really to care deeply for other people and talked in the happiest and most natural way of things which seem to me to matter most." Though she concedes that the fault may have been with herself rather than the Group, she felt the experience was harmful when she attempted to follow a mistaken idea received through "guidance," and was saved from most serious consequences through the personal help of a well-known clergyman. Her sense of the meaning of life was somewhat increased and, for a time, her zest for living; her energies may possibly have been increased. The experience made her more dissatisfied with conventional religion, though her church attendance is still regular. She feels it improved somewhat her moral and ethical habits. It was moderately emotional and added very little to her intellectual equipment except in clarifying some ideas as to what is involved in real Christian living. She gives the following account of what impelled her to join the Group:

From childhood I had an intense interest in religion, religious activities, and religious leaders. During my entire college experience I expected to prepare for the ministry. In spite of all my reading and study, however, I never seemed to find the vital kind of religious faith which would give a real center to my own life and make it possible for me to influence others deeply. Because of my interest in varied expressions of religion, I had known considerable about the Group for a number of years before I became associated with it. The immediate reason for my joining the Wakefield group was my remorse over a fit of anger which seemed to me to indicate that I needed a religion which would more vitally affect my attitudes. It seemed to me that some of the Group members had found a really transforming experience.

While she was not looking forward to a sudden or a startling conversion, she did believe, apart from any idea suggested by the Group, in the necessity for a real Christian's going through a transformation, gradual or sudden, "by which God or Christ becomes the center of life and desire rather than self." Her attitude toward the Group is still very sympathetic and appreciative as "an attempt to meet the very real need for spiritual fellowship and a vital personal religion." The dangers which turned her from it were (1) the tendency to follow too literally injurious ideas in the guise of divine guidance; (2) the tendency to pride and exhibitionism in recounting religious experience; (3) the occasional violation of personality in overzealous attempts to "change" people. In addition, as a pacifist, she feels that what she hears of the Group's war program is inconsistent with its principles. But with respect to the common criticism of the Group's overemphasis on sex, she says that in her experience she never heard it mentioned in public testimony nor did she ever see any indication of abnormal interest in it.

Besides being very full, this testimony is interesting as a fairly recent experience with the Group. But it is chiefly interesting as describing a patently sincere effort to absorb just what the Group has to offer, which nevertheless failed because of characteristic weaknesses in the Group program and technique. Here is a case where a deeply religious nature longed for a means of vitalizing her religious faith, expressing aspirations that lay deeply within her, and influencing others for good. These needs the Group met for a time, but a too-literal reliance on "guidance" almost led to a personal tragedy, and this served to undermine her confidence in the movement. One is inclined to credit Miss Robertson's charity and forbearance for her statement that it might have been her fault. But wherever the fault lay, here is a case where a person of sincerity and religious depth failed to find permanent satisfaction with the Group.

Curtis Brown

In 1920, when an undergraduate, Curtis Brown attended a meeting at Oxford University at which Dr. Buchman spoke. His interest was very warm and appreciative, and he says, "I wanted to be active, but not having any dramatic leadership ability I was never given the chance." His family was in very moderate circumstances, and his training had been strongly religious. He has always been regular in church attendance. Before his contact with the Group he had been dissatisfied with regard to a sex problem and a previous conversion experience that was becoming less vivid. He thought the Group offered a way of keeping it permanent. He is now a parish clergyman.

Originally he felt the experience to be deeply religious and still feels it had genuine religious values, but is now more inclined to credit obvious needs and enthusiasms with distorting it. The experience had both beneficial and harmful effects. It helped him to become a better mixer and "to take a less narrow view on certain things," though he feels he should have gotten these things in other ways. He does not specify the harmful effects except to say that they were present. He now has no contact with the Group and does not think it has any great contribution for him, though he admires Dr. Buchman's efforts to revive evangelical religion.

Brown's case is kept out of the Neutral group, on the one hand, by the warmth of his initial experience, from the Positive group, on the other, by the comparative slightness of the effects upon him. One may speculate that the latter is accounted for by the lack of a chance to express his experience through leadership and activity in the Group. If so, he chiefly illustrates the need for some kind of expression if this kind of religious experience is to have lasting benefit.

E. M. Blackwell

E. M. Blackwell was a student in theological school in 1924 when a clergyman introduced him to the Oxford Group. His mother had recently died, and he had been in general dissatisfied with his life, so the fellowship of the Group made a great appeal to him. He was active with the Group for about a year. His family was in very moderate circumstances, and he reports them as only nominally religious, yet he had expected a conversion before contact with the Group. He is now an Episcopal clergyman.

He is not sure how genuine he felt the experience to be at the time, but now he looks on the death of his mother as the factor that made him susceptible to the Group's influence. The movement met his need for fellowship and improved his moral and ethical life at the seminary. The experience was likewise harmful, he thinks, in the encouragement to lean heavily on intuition and emotion. He now feels friendly toward the movement but is doubtful of its real worth.

This seems to be a clear case of a young man who met the Group at a critical time in his life when he needed help and companionship. Through the fellowship it afforded, this need was satisfied, and very likely this tided him over a difficult period. But again its intellectual poverty and emotional content was somewhat harmful, so that, despite his active interest, Blackwell was not held in the movement for more than a year.

Chapter Fifteen

The Positive Cases

Samuel Hoffman

Samuel Hoffman is at present an Episcopal clergyman whose experience with the Group was almost wholly favorable. He attended a well-known boy's school and a large New England university, and first came in contact with the Group at the age of about twenty-five when in business more than fifteen years ago. He reports himself as "changed" and an active worker in the Group for thirteen years. His own income is reported as moderate at the time. He describes his mother as having strong religious faith, the other members of his family as not so religious but active in altruistic enterprise.

Hoffman is very positive about the religious reality of the experience. He says, "Nothing else could have done the same in me—or through me, in subsequent years." It "gave direction, purpose; showed me The One Thing worth giving your life for." The experience was felt to be "beneficial in every way." It gave him his first sense of religious certainty; and that experience has continued to be an increasing reality. It gave new awareness of the meaning and value of life, and a new direction for energies and zest for living. He believes his attitude toward life was changed constructively by the experience, that without it he would probably have continued a divided person, self-centered, feeling rather useless; instead of having "the one thing most needed by individuals and the world." His habits of church attendance before the experience were only those required in church schools "and a curious or hungry visit to Church once in a while." His replies are uniformly and enthusiastically positive. It seems clear that the experience made him a much more dynamic person. For the first time he realized he might have latent qualities of leadership, and "in personal interviews lives were changed or helped." He rejoiced in finding himself "an influence for good instead of just a 'nice fellow.' " He does not make it clear that the movement added to his intellectual equipment as such, but his replies indicate that this was so at least indirectly in that it "clarified and unified" his thinking, stimulated further study, and led to his entering the theological seminary. He reports the experience as "naturally and rightly attended with some emotion," but adds that he has been a far less emotional person ever since. Before his contact with the Group he was "uncertain about life work . . . divided." Nothing in previous church or school training had led him to expect a religious conversion; that experience he thought of as "something that happened only in rescue missions" until his reading of Begbie's *More Twice-Born Men* suggested its possibility for him. He has now withdrawn from the Group, and while he feels he owes much to it, he deplores its present intolerance and narrowness. He believes it leans too much toward dictatorship in its unconscious organization and has departed from its early Christ-centered program. Yet he believes very much in the need and reality of conversion, and wishes it were "the natural and expected experience" for upper-class Americans.

This reply was among the most positive received. The integrating quality of the experience is obvious; it directed him toward the ministry after a period of floundering around. Released from self-interest, he has found his greatest interest in other people. His earlier reading and studies in psychology were given life and motivation both as applied to his own life and in dealing with others; "in Christ I found the expulsive power of a new affection." Along with this integration have come increased energy and motivation; he is loyal to his church as the instrument of his aims. In summary we may say that here we have an example of a person for whom the experience, personally, was wholly fortunate and happy.

Harriss Wood

Harriss Wood's wealthy family was only nominally religious. He was sent to a fashionable church school and a large university, after which he became an investment banker. Yet he was dissatisfied with life "in almost every way." Far from expecting conversion he "didn't know it was possible," but at the age of forty in 1934 he sought out the Group where, at his first contact, the testimony and evidence of others introduced the idea to him. He was "changed" and for several years was active in the movement.

This he has looked on as "an entirely new experience resulting in miracles—explainable only by the supernatural." The results were harmful in no way. The experience "changed point of view and values, also the power to put them into effect as I am willing to call on this power." It increased his religious certainty, meaning of life, zest for living, and energies. He yet is not a regular church-goer, though before he never went at all. It improved his moral and ethical habits, gave him an interest in other people, gave him the power to deal with his own problems, and increased his control over his sexual life, though this is still a problem. It improved his mental equipment in that he now sees his problems clearly, can articulate them, and knows the answers. He feels that emotion played a moderate part. With respect to the movement at present he says, "The M.R.A. angle has spoiled it all—the M.R.A. leaders (Buchman, etc.) have scuttled it, but Shoemaker, etc., have returned to the real thing—personal religion that works."

Here is a case of genuine conversion typical of that fostered by the Group in that the focus of it is the solution of personal problems. Wood does not specify very exactly, but probably the vices of his class such as sexual indulgence, drinking, and perhaps occasional unethical business practices had so complicated his life that it had become all but unbearable. The Group has here salvaged a man who was very likely on his way to becoming a useless citizen. The tone of his replies indicates that not only his moral but also his mental health has improved, and the experience has lasted long enough to indicate that its effects may well be permanent.

Frederick Moorman

Frederick Moorman's family was fashionable and very well off, with average religious interests. He was in his last year of graduate school in 1925 and living at rather a fast pace but dissatisfied with his life, when he was coaxed by some friends into attending an Oxford Group Houseparty. He had not thought of conversion before, but here he experienced a "sudden and cataclysmic conversion" and thereafter was very active in the Group for the period of a year. Subsequently he entered the Episcopal priesthood.

He still feels his experience to have been genuinely religious, though he now understands more clearly psychological factors which led up to and colored it. The results were almost wholly beneficial. "I started to lead a more unselfish and disciplined life and ultimately came to the ministry." The experience increased his religious certainty, the meaning of life, his zest for living, and his energies. It gave him his "first appreciation of forgiveness and of personal salvation." Rarely present at church before, he afterward attended regularly. It led to his stopping drinking, improved his sex behavior, and increased his capacity to deal with his own personal problems. It is interesting to note that he refused to stop smoking, not thinking it a sin, despite the attitude of some of the leaders. The experience was harmful "only in so far as it made me at the time priggish and intolerant, and fostered a certain spiritual pride." But it also affected his studies in that he cut his classes to attend Houseparties. The movement added nothing to his intellectual equipment and was largely emotional, though this is not to his mind a condemnation. With respect to the Group at present he says, "The program is inadequate for a full religious life. It practically ignores the sacraments. I object to the playing up of titles and prominent people. Its terminology is cant."

As in the previous case of Harriss Wood, it again appears that the Group took hold of a young man well on his way toward an unsatisfactory, dissipated life complicated by sexual problems, and not only turned him toward a disciplined, ordered existence but was even responsible for his entering the ministry. He would probably illustrate what Buchman has in mind when he refers to his work among the "up-and-outs." No doubt the unconscious sense of disorder about his life had led Moorman to become dissatisfied, so that the example of others who testified to lives of meaning through Group discipline made a strong appeal. The relief consequent on the conversion released strong emotional forces, and the practice and discipline fostered by successive Houseparties were sufficient to make his new attitudes habitual. But very likely the Group's organizational and doctrinal shortcomings along with its too great dependence on emotion palled on him at last so that he left it, eventually for a religious life with more ecclesiastical emphasis which at the same time preserved the values and attitudes he originally owed to the Group.

Samuel Smith

Samuel V. Smith, Jr. came from a well-to-do, religious background. He has always attended church regularly and he believed in the possibility of conversion. When a junior at college in 1925, he was bothered by certain sexual anxieties and the lack of a definite aim in life. Through friends he attended one or two Oxford Group Houseparties where his experience was warm and appreciative. But he was never at all active, due to certain reservations he had at the time. He now is a teacher of Bible and English at a preparatory school.

He then felt the experience genuinely religious, and still does, though he now feels it more understandable. Its influence was beneficial in that it "(1) allayed certain sexual anxieties; (2) stimulated emotional life and ideals mostly in what I consider healthy ways; (3) gave me an insight into the realities of the religious life; (4) furthered personal integration." It increased his sense of religious certainty, the meaning of life, and his energies. It affected his attitudes in that it "sharpened my sense of the reality of spiritual values. Was one of the factors that led me into teaching." It was beneficial to his moral and ethical habits, also his hobbies or interests—he says his present interest in religious psychology is due to it. It improved his attitude toward sex, but he is not sure of its effect on his capacity to deal with his personal problems. The experience added nothing to his intellectual equipment and was largely emotional "but a value I needed at the time." The only way in which it was harmful was that it "may have overstimulated ideals without provision for follow-up." He believes that the Group supplies "emotional and volitional values" needed in present-day religion. However, he thinks the movement has gone astray lately due to the lack of any real intellectual background and the "dictatorial leanings of Buchman."

Smith's experience is somewhat unusual in that it was so universally beneficial without his ever having been committed to the movement. But the results are somewhat milder than those in the two previous cases, which involved definite conversion. Apparently he is of a somewhat thoughtful turn, as indicated by his interest in religious psychology, and to this side the Group made no direct appeal—which may explain his reservations at the time of the experience. On the other hand, the Group did help his sexual attitudes and helped fulfill his need for vocational integration. His increased sense of the "reality of spiritual values" no doubt satisfied certain religious cravings, and he indicates it is an aid to him in his teaching of literature. In summary, the Group successfully fulfilled Smith's need for moral and, to a certain extent, vocational guidance, while at the same time it deepened his spiritual life.

Harold Counts

Harold Counts' family were strongly religious, liberal-thinking Congregationalists in moderate circumstances. He was sent to a well-known small college where as a freshman of eighteen in 1924 he attended an Oxford Group Houseparty. He had not been conscious of any dissatisfaction with his life "except a vague pricking of conscience on certain matters" and had "no intelligent expectation of a conversion." However, "through conviction of personal sin and a desire to 'live clean,' " he experienced what he calls a "moral conversion," which touched his personal life but not his theology. He was active for three years, after which he entered a theological seminary. He is now a Baptist minister with Fundamentalist convictions.

At the time he felt the experience genuinely religious. At present he says, "I am a stronger believer than ever in the supernatural elements of true Christianity, but I now consider the Oxford Group very shallow. Much of their mysticism is produced by psychological means." Actually the experience had only beneficial results. It was "beneficial morally at that period of adolescence and freedom from home ties and restraints. Its emphasis on 'quiet times' led me to read the

Bible for myself, which I would not otherwise have done." While the experience did not increase his sense of religious certainty, it did increase the meaning of life, his zest for living, and his energies. He considers the experience the start of his personal religious life but says, "it might not have been permanent if additional outside influences had not given me a solid intellectual foundation for my faith." His church attendance, which had become "very spasmodic when away from home," became "quite regular." With respect to his social life at college he says, "I was considered quite an extremist in that I quit smoking and dancing, but it did not hurt me any." The experience made him more serious in his studies, led him to go into the ministry, improved his moral and ethical habits, increased his capacity to deal with his own personal problems by giving him belief in prayer, and increased his control over his sexual life. Yet he observes, "It might have been harmful if I had not received a genuine instruction in the Bible and in sound doctrine from other sources." The movement added to his intellectual equipment "only in that it started me studying the Bible." He considers the experience to have been moderately emotional.

Paradoxically, despite its benefits to him, Counts strongly condemns the movement as "the devil's method of sidetracking Christians into a social service and humanitarian program instead of seeking the salvation of their souls for eternity." Also he has noticed that many "changes" were temporary because of the lack of sound doctrinal teaching, in which case they were more harmful than otherwise in turning persons away from religion. In addition, he objects to open confessions on the score that repeated repetitions make sins more tolerable.

Counts' case is interesting in that, from an entirely different viewpoint, he confirms the criticism of others who feel the movement weak because of its intellectual and doctrinal shortcomings. Also he illustrates the importance of early training in the experience, since his father was a minister. Very likely the "vague prickings of conscience" to which he refers can be traced to his childhood training, while the means of assuaging them was found in the Group. In this connection it is significant that as a result of his conversion he "quit smoking and dancing." Here it is interesting to compare his case with that of Moorman, who was just as definitely converted but, with quite a different background, refused to give up smoking as a sin despite the disapproval of other members of the Group. In summary we may venture the surmise that in Counts' case the Oxford Group was the means of vitalizing ingrained religious forces which, once awakened, demanded not only expression but rationalization. The need for the latter was not satisfied by the Group, so Counts left it to work out his own theology, which led him to his present Fundamentalist convictions, and the Baptist Church. This now colors his attitude toward the Group.

Samuel Cunningham

Samuel Cunningham's family was in very moderate circumstances and of average religious interests. He went to a large university and then theological school, where he was dissatisfied with his life when Dr. Buchman visited the campus in 1924. He had not expected conversion but through "continuous contact with inspired converted personalities" he was "changed" and was active in the Group for a period of fifteen years. He is now an Episcopalian clergyman.

Today he looks on the experience as the result of "true spiritual influences explainable only by reference to God," which had only beneficial results. He says, "It has given point and purpose to my ministry and stability to my whole life, and courage to carry on in the face of otherwise insurmountable difficulties." It heightened his sense of religious certainty, the meaning of life, his zest for living and his energies. With respect to his attitudes he says, "It has revealed to me areas of life that the church, *per se,* has not reached, my own life and that of others. It has made a confirmed optimist out of a person inclined to be the opposite." It was beneficial to his social life in the seminary, gave certainty to his already-made choice of the ministry, and was likewise beneficial to his moral and ethical habits, his interests, his capacity to deal with his own problems and his attitude toward sex. It added to his intellectual equipment in that it "taught me the need of intellectual honesty and correlated all my intellectual activity." He feels it to have been moderately emotional.

Of the movement today he says, "I am as firm a believer as ever in its principles and loyal to its leaders. Some of its present methods I regard as a departure from the spiritual genius of the movement."

While there was little hint in Cunningham's replies of what specific needs led him to the Group, it is clear that the result illustrates the integration of a personality through a religious experience and consequent loyalty to a cause. This has given him direction, improved his mental, spiritual, and, one suspects, his physical health besides. Even his intellectual activity has been correlated with his spiritual purpose. Whether the intellectual raw materials came from within or without the movement he does not say, and probably could not. His experience has so possessed his whole life that it has reached out and compassed all his experiences so that they seem one. The only hint of a critical attitude is in his questioning of some of the present methods of the Group. But his own experience is too vivid and real for him any longer to be dependent on the policies of the movement.

Perry Abbott

Perry Abbott came from a strongly religious family in moderate circumstances. He had been converted before the age of twenty-nine when, in 1918, he met Dr. Buchman. At this time he was a student in theological school and dissatisfied with his own spiritual ineffectiveness. He says, "Frank Buchman showed me how to put into action truths I had long believed." After this he was active in the Group for twenty years. He is now a Presbyterian minister.

He says, "The whole experience was a real and vital one which still lasts . . . not only beneficial but radical—It gave me the spiritual experience I'd been looking for . . . gave me the tools to do a job." His answers to detailed items indicate an experience that was uniformly positive. Of its intellectual influence he says, "It helped me to face facts." He calls it "normally" emotional.

But with respect to the movement he says the following:

> I feel that they have forsaken their early methods and objectives. . . . I am as strongly convinced today as I was in the early part of my experience that the Oxford Group of ten or fifteen years ago was the most potent spiritual movement within the Church of Christ that our generation has seen.
>
> I believe that in the last few years the objectives and the methods of the Group have changed. I feel they are no longer a movement within the Church and that their objectives are not the objectives which Christ left with His Church. Nor can I follow them in their methods. There is in my own mind a great difference between the "Oxford Group" and "Moral Re-Armament."

Here is an example of a sensitive religious nature who found spiritual effectiveness through the Group. It may be questioned to what extent the ability to face facts is an intellectual attribute, as he seems to feel, rather than a moral one; though no doubt it has its intellectual application. But Abbott primarily illustrates the invigorating effect that the Group had on a religious life.

Millman Davis

Millman Davis became interested in the Group when at college in 1920. His family was very well-to-do and had sent him to an expensive preparatory school. He had grown up with people who had expected and encouraged conversion, so that previously he had gone through several experiences; yet he was "changed" through the Group despite previous general satisfaction with his life. He says, "It was the rigorousness of the appeal to give my life to God no matter what happened which effected a revaluation of a fairly dynamic but complacent life." He worked intimately with the Group for three years, when he broke off from the movement "because of what I considered its metaphysical naïveté and theological superficiality." He is now a Congregational minister connected with both a theological seminary and a boys' school.

He originally felt the experience to be genuinely religious and still believes in guidance, though with certain reservations. On the whole he feels the experience to have been beneficial. "It certainly caught me up sharply on the idea that a Christian ought to submit his decisions to meditation in the light of his belief in the reality of God and the purposes of Christ." It increased his sense of religious certainty, the meaning of life, his zest for living and his energies. It affected his attitude toward life constructively. "Although I was a fairly 'good boy' in the conventional sense before (no smoking, drinking, sex irregularities), the conversion experience gave me the conviction that it is important to take one's life decisions with serious earnestness—religion included." The latter led to his decision for the ministry—the chief fruit of the experience. With respect to ethics and morals he says, "It made me more sensitive about honesty of speech, thoroughness, spending money, minor sex matters—although a bit Pharisaical." It probably increased his capacity to deal with his personal problems, "but

I tended to solve them on a 'guidance' basis without enough hard thinking and advice of experienced non-Buchmanites." He says it was harmful "possibly in the attitude toward sex which I was forced to assume for a while; that is, a somewhat unpsychological and totally moralistic attitude. A good deal of unnecessary tension was maintained at this point." He also says, "I think I became a bit Pharasaical and exhibitionist in my belief that those who did not agree with me were entirely wrong, and I liked to tell the story of my own conversion too much." With respect to his old friends still in the Group he says, "Recently I have just let them alone, as they always tried (rather obviously) to 'work on' me to get me back, under the guise of innocent friendly approaches; like classmates who try to sell you life insurance."

Davis' testimony is particularly convincing as an unusually thorough and critical piece of introspection. Again the Group is shown as doing an excellent job of spiritual vitalization. Davis presented a particularly adequate evangelistic religious background on which the Group built. He had already experienced conversions, but apparently the Group was the first force which took hold of him effectually. With his excellent mind and talents he might easily have become successful in a field of endeavor other than the ministry had it not been for the Group. It does not appear that he felt any compelling need for the experience, for he indicates that his life was dynamic and active before, and he was not dissatisfied with it. Apparently, however, the challenge to take his Christian professions seriously caught his imagination and lifted him to what he feels to have been a higher and more satisfying plane. But again the Group failed to satisfy a keen mind, and the movement was left behind, though not the benefits and changed attitudes it had brought to the emotional and volitional sides of his religious life. Davis illustrates admirably both the strengths and some of the weaknesses of the movement. Yet the influence on him was predominantly beneficial.

Peter Eliot

Peter Eliot's background was well-to-do and strongly religious. While at preparatory school at the age of seventeen he first came into contact with the Group, which, around 1920, was active at a neighboring college. He feels that it appealed to his need for integration, and within two or three years, after he had gone to college, his interest grew very warm and appreciative though not "changed." He was active for about a year and a half. Now he is a Presbyterian minister.

He feels that the experience was genuinely religious "although I did not then nor do I now feel that the Group techniques were the heart of it." What effect the Group had on him he considers wholly beneficial. Along with his religious background and academic study it was one of the influences that led to his choosing the ministry, and he is still thankful for the challenge and the friendship of some of the leaders. He feels that it furthered the integration of his life even though in the end this integration was not directed toward the movement. It was beneficial to his moral and ethical habits and his capacity to deal with his personal problems. Intellectually the movement gave him little "except by way of reaction." The experiment was largely emotional, but he believes all religion must have emotion. His opinion of the Group is that it has done much good and some harm.

Eliot feels that the Group helped to answer his need for personal integration, though it was not the only influence involved in this process. Like others he speaks of the challenge of the Group and its fellowship. Yet his experience was not as intense as many; and it is noteworthy that he recognizes his religious experience which, combined with the largely emotional emphasis of the Group, formed a well-rounded whole.

Bertha Mann

Bertha Mann was training to be a nurse when, in 1920, at the age of twenty-four, she was introduced to Dr. Buchman. Her family was in moderate circumstances and strongly religious. She had already had a conversion experience and was not dissatisfied with her life, for she says, "I definitely believed that I had dedicated myself before meeting the Group." But her experience was nevertheless warm and appreciative, and for six years she was active in the Group. During this period she entered theological school and is now an ordained minister.

Originally Miss Mann felt the experience genuinely religious; now she feels that some of it was due to the "contagion of personalities or (social) group experiences." It was beneficial chiefly in teaching her "the value and need of leading or helping others to know God and the Christ—not to be afraid to speak of religion or to share mine. Somehow I had not learned this as a personal fact from church or home." It increased the meaning of life and her zest for living, and while it did not increase her energies, it helped direct them into missionary channels. In her social contacts it made her less self-conscious. She does not feel it to have been harmful "perhaps because I withdrew when I found myself growing away from its methods and beliefs." It added nothing to her intellectual equipment and was moderately emotional. Her attitude toward the Group is now "interested, sympathetic, appreciative of the experiences I had with it and of the help it is rendering many people now but do not agree with all its methods or fundamentalist beliefs."

Apparently Miss Mann's religious life was already pretty well integrated before her contact with the Group. Consequently, the latter heightened and changed somewhat its direction without altering its fundamental quality. Chiefly it aroused and directed her missionary interests and, in helping her to overcome her self-consciousness and enabling her to talk more freely about religion, it implemented those interests. This then would be a case to illustrate, among other things, a fairly common characteristic of the Group influence in encouraging people to speak more freely of their own religious lives.

Noel Bridgeman

Noel Bridgeman was a member of a family prominent in liberal religious circles. After graduating from an American college he attended an English university where, about 1920, he met Dr. Buchman. He was very much dissatisfied with his life, and, though not expecting conversion, he was eventually "changed" through seeing and hearing about conversion from others, For fifteen years, though particularly when the Group was small, he was very active in it. He is now an Episcopal clergyman.

Of his connection with the Group he says:

> It was a true and lasting religious experience. It gave me an inner unity, taught me that God has a plan for my life, helped me to find it, led me to find God's help in meeting moral difficulties, made the message of the Church become alive and real, led me into a remarkable fellowship with other people . . . taught me much about helping others . . . and changed my attitude most constructively. It made me feel at once a part of life and not merely an onlooker. It brought me out of myself to feel the call of the Kingdom of God.

The experience increased his sense of religious certainty, the meaning of life, his zest for living, and his energies. All features noted on the questionnaire were indicated as being benefitted by the experience with the exception of hobbies and interests, after which he comments "no time for them, but they were not important." Intellectually he says it "enormously increased my interest in Theology and Church History, etc., and helped to break many old moulds of thought." He feels emotion played "a proper part. It was the result of my experience, not the cause of it." Of the Group today he says:

> Its leader, desiring to find an outlet of activity for the many changed lives the movement produced and failing to find it in the Church, has become too much absorbed in a world program, creating an organization in fact, though not in appearance, and gradually allowing the means to be sacrificed to the end.

The effect of this experience was universally happy and beneficial with no harmful results. While Bridgeman does not specify in what ways he was dissatisfied before his conversion, one may infer from his testimony that it was in a lack of integrated purpose and very likely a sense of unreality in connection with the Christian professions to which he had been brought up. No doubt trained to have a very sensitive conscience, he was disturbed by moral difficulties which he had been powerless to overcome; and perhaps he also felt a need to share inner religious activity that diffidence led him to keep to himself. The Group afforded an opportunity and supplied the power to satisfy his deep-seated needs. As a result, the call of Christian service has possessed his whole being—a service in which the Group was a means, not an end, for very likely his conception of the Kingdom of God was absorbed during his youth more than it was formed through the Group movement. At any rate, the result of this possession was a unity of personality which embraces even his hobbies and interests. Many clergymen, for example, would consider an interest in theology and church history a desirable but by no means an obligatory exercise for a pastor; but this does not occur to

Bridgeman, for he looks on it as part of his work. It might be questioned whether this interest, which he ascribes to the movement, may not be due to his own particular reaction to the experience, since the Group emphasizes neither theology nor church history. Fundamentally, however, we have illustrated here the vitalization of religion through the Group with consequent integration of personality.

Caroline Grant

Caroline Grant's family was very well-to-do and had average religious interests. After finishing school she describes herself as having little purpose and being very undecided, and she was looking for a deeper religious experience than she could get through teaching a Sunday school class and going to church. Otherwise she was not particularly dissatisfied with her life and was not expecting conversion. In 1925, however, she became interested in the Group through girls' meetings as well as through theological students she knew. She was "changed" through the reading of such books as Begbie's *More Twice-Born Men,* H. A. Walter's *Soul Surgery,* and James' *Varieties of Religious Experience,* combined with hearing the witness of people in meetings. She is now married to a clergyman. She and her husband have been very active in the Group until very recently when they withdrew because they felt they could not support Moral Re-Armament.

She gives the following testimony with respect to her experience:

I know my experience to have been genuine. I believe it to be only explainable with reference to God, with the help and direction of others who had been helped themselves. . . . It gave me purpose and direction in my life, a sense of freedom and resolving of conflicts. It also gave me a most helpful and enjoyable fellowship of similarly interested people and a training and experience in trying to help others which is invaluable; above all it gave me experience of religion which has stood by me.

The experience increased her sense of religious certainty, the meaning of life, zest for living, and energies. Her attitudes were changed permanently in a constructive way. "The realization that God has a plan for every life gives purpose to life and interest." The experience had a beneficial effect on her vocational choice, moral and ethical habits, hobbies and interests, capacity to deal with her own problems, and her attitude toward sex. There was nothing harmful about it. With respect to intellectual equipment she says, "I read a good number of books on religious, social, and psychological subjects, and thought and talked a great deal about those subjects. I worked in two churches and learned about the church, which has been of great value to me ever since." She feels emotion played a slight part: "I think it must have some part as well as the intellect and spirit." Of the movement she says:

> I feel that the movement has spread thin, possibly through ambition on some of the leaders' part. Most of the members are sincere and some are doing fine work. I cannot agree with some of their methods of publicity nor some of their training and I cannot conform to much of their thinking. Conformity seems to be more demanded than it used to be. My husband and I are not actively associated with MRA.

Mrs. Grant apparently has an intrinsically religious nature, for despite only average religious upbringing she nevertheless longed for deeper religious experience than her contact with the church had given her. The Group satisfied this longing through an experience that integrated her life and brought with it the numerous other benefits she enumerates above. In general this is another definite and clear-cut illustration of religion made vital through the Group.

Samuel Endicott

Samuel Endicott's family was wealthy, socially prominent, intelligent, and strongly religious. Trained as an engineer, Endicott had decided to go into the ministry, feeling that in this field he could make a more fundamental contribution to society. He was already in the seminary when he first came in contact with the Group about 1920. In answering the question as to whether he was dissatisfied with his life he says, "I hope so, and hope I still am." He had not been led to expect a religious conversion; now he looks on conversion as one, but not the only road to the spiritual life. His interest in the Group grew gradually, until about six years later it was "warm and appreciative." He was never very active, "on 'near fringes' for two or three years; before and after that on 'far fringes.' " He is now the headmaster of a Southern church school for boys.

He has always felt the experience to be genuinely religious, which feeling has not been lessened by the fact that he can now explain much "guidance" as the distillation of the subconscious or as simple common sense. It was definitely beneficial in helping to free him from certain inhibitions and in supplying him with a technique for more direct and effective work with individuals. He says that it did "not much" increase his sense of religious certainty and the meaning of life; but probably increased his zest for living and energies. It was somewhat beneficial to his social life in the seminary through "reduction of some fruitless inhibitions"; and it was also of some help to his capacity to deal with his personal problems, though he was more conscious of help in dealing with others. With respect to sex he says, "Personally for me this was mostly a tempest in a teapot." For him the movement had no harmful results.

The movement had "almost no intellectual influence on me,

except indirectly that such an eminent scholar as Streeter should 'fall for it.' " Emotion played a part in his experience "moderately or largely." He has the following to say of his present attitude:

> Rather anti. Political and theological attitudes seem non-constructive. High power publicity—playing up big names—and general snobbish exclusiveness is rather revolting. I object very much to lack of even the simple fundamentals of honesty, though absolute honesty is one of the corner-stones. I believe at my school that a *majority* of those parents having close contact with the movement were somewhere between financially dishonest to thoughtlessly and inconsiderately casual. . . .
>
> I believe there is real power in any *group* endeavor marked by earnestness and a common outlook. This tones up, temporarily at least, one's zest of living, and releases energies which in a purely individual undertaking would probably not be present. But this is what the Christian Church has always stood for, though often it has not got it across. . . .
>
> My chief objection is the exclusiveness implicit in the widespread feeling of the Group that it is the *only* way.

Endicott's experience was much milder than the average in the Positive group. He apparently always has had reservations, while his early interest in engineering suggests that his mind runs to the theoretical and technical, to which a more intellectual approach to religion than that of the Group would have an appeal. Consequently it was the technique of the Group that interested him, and this he adapted to his own uses in his work as a minister and educator. On the other hand, his experience did involve emotion; very likely the reduction of his inhibitions was one of the fruits of this. His critical faculty no doubt prevented the experience from being as profound as in some of the other Positive cases, but at the same time it saved him from excesses with attendant harmful reactions.

Chapter Sixteen

The Positive Cases *(continued)*

William Marshall

William Marshall came from a strongly religious Quaker background. His family was in very moderate circumstances when, as a college student in 1924, he attended an Oxford Group Houseparty. He had not been dissatisfied with his life, nor had his training led him to expect conversion, yet his interest was very warm though not active. He is now an Episcopalian and in business.

He originally felt the experience to be genuinely religious, while now he finds the question more difficult to answer; but he does not think that "guidance" can necessarily be explained away. In general the experience had little influence on him either way, though he indicates it was beneficial to his social life in college and to his studies. It was somewhat harmful in that it strengthened a feeling of vocation for the priesthood, when now he realizes that he was not definitely called. It added nothing to his intellectual equipment and was moderately emotional. He now has no strong feeling either for or against the movement.

Marshall's involvement was so slight that he might have been classed with the Neutral group. Nevertheless his interest had been warm, and what effects there were were mostly beneficial. Very likely his religious background gave him an interest in activities such as the Oxford Group's, which for a time made his religion more vivid.

SIDNEY BUSHNELL

Sidney Bushnell was forty years old, in business, and moderately well off when he first came in contact with the Oxford Group at a church meeting in 1932. His background had been strongly religious, and he had been dissatisfied with his life in that he "saw no way to clear up certain mistakes and lacked sense of direction." He had recognized the possibility of conversion but did not expect it until the idea came to him through personal witness of other people like himself. As a consequence he was "changed" and was active with the Group for six years. He is a Congregationalist and at present a branch manager for a prominent manufacturing concern.

He believes his experience to have been "genuinely spiritual, similar to conversion." He says it gave new direction to his life, made spiritual values a dominant influence, and brought his entire family closer together, giving him a greater sense of comradeship with his children. It stimulated Bible study, family prayers, and started the habit of morning quiet. It increased his sense of religious certainty, the meaning of life, his zest for living, and energies. His habits of church attendance, already quite regular, became more so and at the same time more appreciative and worshipful. The experience was beneficial to his studies, moral and ethical habits, interests, his capacity to deal with his personal problems, and his attitude toward sex. There were no harmful results. He feels that it added to his intellectual equipment "by training in quiet thinking through of problems after prayer and in the attitude of seeking God's leading in seeking his solution to problems." Emotion played a moderate part. He makes the following comments on the Group:

I feel deeply indebted to it and them [its leaders]. I regret that they have become so anxious for quick results and large numbers that in "Moral Re-Armament" they have come to use high pressure sales methods, lacking honesty, and make constant use of names of prominent people not actually identified with the movement in such a way as to mislead people.

The Oxford Group had in it the germ of new life for our churches and emphasized points which our churches, especially the Protestant church, have been neglecting. The influence of quiet—the emphasis on a continual "changing" rather than a one time conversion—the possibility of divine guidance—the soundness of confession—the value of sharing (under prayer and guidance). All these are like a breath of fresh air in the atmosphere of most churches. Before we can as Christians begin to be effective as a group, we must adopt and put in practice in our lives these "accents" of the Oxford Group at its best.

There is no doubt of the vitality and depth of Bushnell's experience with the Group. The energies released overflowed his entire life, affecting his interests, values, his church experience, and particularly his family life. Perhaps it was his strong religious background that had made him dissatisfied with a conventional businessman's existence involving the usual compromises and leading to the sense of the meaninglessness of such a life. In addition, this may have been heightened by a more or less normal slump in morale involved in the transition from the psychology of young manhood to that of middle age. His case suggests the help that this type of religion may be in bringing new zest and energies to middle-aged people for whom life has settled down to a humdrum, dull, and meaningless round of petty duties and conventional behavior.

The Oxford Group

B. WALLACE INGRAHAM

B. Wallace Ingraham's family was moderately well off and strongly religious. He had always been a regular attendant at church and a leader in young people's work. It was in 1923 during the latter years of his university course when he attended a Houseparty arranged by the college Christian society. He had not thought of conversion except in the case of "down-and-outers," though he was somewhat dissatisfied with his life. He was "vitally interested and deeply affected" by the experience so that for several years following he was active with the Group. He is now a Presbyterian minister and chaplain at a boys' school.

Of his experience he has the following to say:

> I feel that the effort to gain guidance was good—that time taken for meditation and "seeking" to hear what God had to say was important—but that the interpretation of how guidance comes is and was open to serious question. . . . It was a crucial experience for me and at about this time I definitely faced honestly myself, my loyalties, and my willingness really to try to follow Christ's teachings. . . . It gave definite direction and purpose to my life.

In general the effect of the experience was beneficial and vitalizing in every way noted on the questionnaire except that he is not sure of its effect on his hobbies and interests, and he believes that his home, his church, and other factors would have moved him toward his vocation without the added increment of the effect of the Group. However, it increased his interest in church work as well as his attendance. Yet he feels that the experience was largely emotional and added nothing to his intellectual equipment, which was part of the reason why the movement failed to hold his allegiance. He now feels friendly toward it, "but critical of certain of its leaders and of its tendency to make all its members soul surgeons. Herein lies a great danger. Soul surgery is too difficult to trust to naïve and enthusiastic youngsters."

Ingraham's experience is distinguished from many others in the Positive group as a very vital one which yet was recognized as only a minor part of a religious pattern of development which had its real roots in home and church. No doubt this helps to explain its lack of harmful results, despite the fact that it was so largely an emotional affair. His life was not one to require a radical change, though there was some dissatisfaction which, along with a natural interest in religious activities of all kinds, explains the attraction of the Group for him. In it he found the means of challenging, invigorating, and implementing his religious life, which matured through the experience and has been on a higher plane ever since.

Ann Small

Ann Kimball Small was a senior in college in 1920 when she first came in contact with some of the Oxford Group leaders at a student volunteer convention. Her religious training had to some extent led her to expect conversion, and she was dissatisfied with her life at the time. Eventually she was "changed" when attending a Houseparty, where the idea was more strongly presented to her, and for four years after she was fairly active in the Group. Her family was moderately well-to-do at the time. She eventually went into religious work and is now the wife of a Presbyterian minister.

At the time she felt the experience to be genuinely religious, but now as she looks back, many of the issues dealt with seem "superficial and sophomoric." The experience was beneficial in that it "temporarily gave more self-confidence. Loosened me up, helped me to make friends more easily."

Temporarily also, it increased her sense of religious certainty, meaning of life, her zest for living, and energies, though her attitude toward life was not materially changed in any permanent way. The experience was beneficial to her social life in college, her vocational choice in directing her interest toward religious education, and her interests in making her more interested in people. Its chief permanent fruit was a group of very fine, lasting friendships. It may have been slightly harmful in its influence on her sexual attitudes. The experience, she feels, was largely emotional and added nothing in an intellectual way. She now is out of touch with the movement but feels it "too superficial and cocksure. . . . Paradoxical as it may seem, friendships with those who have outgrown the movement seem more lasting than with those who stay active and who keep their cocksure, fanatical, 'holier than thou' attitude."

The results of Mrs. Small's experience were partly ephemeral, but on the other hand they were only slightly harmful. Nevertheless the experience did influence her vocational choice and resulted in some lasting friendships. Despite the fact that the latter continued apart from the Group, the mutual experience was probably responsible for solid foundations, so that we may think of this case as illustrating chiefly the fellowship which the Group affords. Mrs. Small's testimony suggests that the Group met one of her basic needs while at college; namely, companionship, which had formerly been frustrated because of lack of self-confidence and too much reserve. If this was so, it would help to explain her feeling that many of the issues raised at the Houseparties were superficial, because for her they were irrelevant to her real needs and interests. The Group here seems to have done well a job of socialization, and it is through this means that Mrs. Small's religious life has been made more effective.

The Positive Cases

Eunice Herder

Eunice Herder knew Dr. Buchman as early as 1916 when as a young woman of thirty she was secretary to a religious leader. She has been in touch with members of the Group ever since though never active in the movement as such. Her background was religious, and she was interested in the church, but she had never been brought up to believe in sudden conversion. She had what she considers normal Christian dissatisfaction with her life; and though at first irritated, she attended some meetings of the Group and even went so far as to have one confessional interview, which had the effect of quickening her religious life but was not felt to be a conversion. She is an Episcopalian and now holds a supervisory position in a large office.

She feels now, as she did at the time, that the experience was genuinely religious and essentially the same as any true Christian religious experience. She says it "deepened my religious consciousness in some ways; made it possible for me to get across to other people some of the realities of life; deepened my sense of responsibility for helping people. But it is only one of the influences that helped me." The experience was one factor of many which helped to build up a stronger sense of purpose, and some of the leaders of the Group were among the constructive influences in her life. The experience improved her habits of church attendance and her interest in church work. Her regular work was improved; her moral and ethical habits benefitted, and her capacity to deal with her personal problems increased. As a result of the experience she became interested in the subject of mysticism and read much about it. Her reactions were largely dominated by emotion, which she does not feel interfered with their value.

Of her present attitude toward the Group she says:

I am very fond of many of the leaders—immediately feel a friendly interest when I meet one of the Group though at the same time I know I am an outsider. Their slogans and high-pressure methods always irritate me, but the deep Christian character of my particular friends makes me feel humble.

In addition she lists as features she objects to (1) slogans and cant, (2) lack of sense of humor, (3) lack of appreciation of the work of the Christian Church, and (4) tendency to believe that people have never experienced changed lives unless they say so in the language of the Group. On the other hand she appreciates (1) the sincerity of many of the members, (2) the fact that even some of the methods she dislikes enable the Group to reach people otherwise inaccessible to religion, (3) the Group's real ability to help people, and (4) the sense of unity present in the "quiet times."

For Miss Herder the Group was simply one of many influences which stimulated her religious development. She is notable as a woman who, though her main religious focus is the Church and though she is irritated by much connected with the Group, is nevertheless broadminded enough to recognize and appreciate many of its praiseworthy features.

Carlton Brooks

Though Carlton Brooks' family was in moderate circumstances, he attended a prominent preparatory school and an Eastern college, finishing his education as a Rhodes Scholar at Oxford. He had been brought up in a strongly religious atmosphere but was not expecting a conversion. At the time of his first contact with the Group, as a freshman in college in 1923, he was troubled by indecision about his career. His attitude gradually underwent a transformation, and finally he "surrendered." From 1931 to 1938 he was at times active in the movement. He is now an Episcopal clergyman and the headmaster of a New England boys' school.

He looks on his experience as definitely religious:

> Guidance is a real and continuing experience and the discipline and fellowship of the Group was, to me, a sound and valid religious experience. It gave me deeper insight into the Christian religion, and a completeness of challenge not given by any other group or human agency.

It increased his sense of religious certainty, the meaning of life, and his zest for living, though not his energies. He says, "It enhanced and developed rather than 'changed' my religious attitude." It was beneficial to his vocational choice, moral and ethical habits, his capacity to deal with his own problems, and his attitude toward sex. It was in no way harmful. Intellectually it "gave me deeper insight into the Bible and God's plan revealed there," while emotion played a moderate part. He is now deeply grateful to the movement for what it has meant to him, though he is not now active in it. "I feel it has made its greatest contribution by quickening the life of the whole church."

Brooks' experience had a quickening and invigorating influence rather than fundamentally changing and converting him. It was very likely this enlivening power that helped him to choose the ministry and so satisfy his need for a vocational decision. Apparently it was his family religious training, his church interests, and the Group influence combined which brought about the decision that otherwise would have led him into something else. The Group, then, is here shown as a factor in turning an able personality toward the ministry as well as being an instrument in deepening his religious experience and so making his ministry worthwhile.

R. Farquhar Kohler

R. Farquhar Kohler came from a wealthy manufacturing family who sent him to the best schools and colleges in this country and abroad. The family religious interests had been only nominal, and he had been brought up to regard conversions as emotional aberrations of the lower classes. However, in 1925, as an undergraduate of eighteen in an Eastern college, he was suffering from the general dissatisfaction of his age in "seeking a purpose in life and wanting to understand 'what it is all about.' " It was then that he came into contact with members of the Oxford Group who showed him "through their approach to the teachings of the New Testament and through showing that a point of decision regarding God and Christ is a natural thing, that conversion is not to be limited to Rescue Missions, revival meetings, and sawdust trails." As a result he was "changed" so that for a ten-year period he was active in the movement. He is now a manufacturing executive in the Middle West and a member of the Presbyterian church.

Of the experience he says:

> I still feel the experience was real. Everyone must consciously or unconsciously choose the direction of his life purposes; self, or God and fellow men. Guidance was and still is for me a real spiritual experience; to me it is facing up to the ultimate realities of life and is deciding questions as they should be decided without personal interest or bias. It is still a factor in decisions, especially major decisions. The experience was beneficial in bringing me to a decision for Christ and teaching me the working of guidance. . . . There was a constructive change in my attitude in that I now try to measure principal decisions as to whether or not they carry out God's will and help fellow men. As a result I am willing to and do serve in many philanthropic activities outside of my business.

It increased his sense of religious certainty, the meaning of life, his zest for living, and his energies. Before, his church attendance was nil, but now it is regular. The experience was beneficial to his moral and ethical habits, his capacity to deal with his own problems, and his attitude toward sex. It was both beneficial and harmful to his vocational choice, while it was harmful to his social life in college, due to the unpopularity of the Group, and it restricted his hobbies and interests. It was also harmful "in that some members got 'guidance' for me and led me to decisions before I had all the facts; hence I made a few bad and important decisions . . . and maybe even that was not too harmful." He mentions nothing that it added to his intellectual equipment, but indicates that it was moderately emotional, which he feels is normal and proper in the light of the depth of the experience.

Of the movement at present he says:

> I have lost contact since it became "Moral Re-Armament." Could never feel "F.B." [Buchman] as a real Christian leader. Believe they are now well away from the "First Century Christian Fellowship" idea. My separation started when they began to insist on my accepting "Group Guidance"—this idea is *very* dangerous.

This experience might have been classed as Partly Positive since there were some harmful effects. Nevertheless Kohler seems to feel that these were rather limited, and his testimony is in other respects so definite as to warrant classification as Positive. Before coming in contact with the Group he apparently was conscious of the need for something which would make life worthwhile. He had not been very religious and very likely felt little or no obligation toward his Christian faith, as was not the case with most others of the Positive group. But the Oxford Group way of living seemed to give purpose to his life. It was a true educational influence in that it introduced him to the values and the possibilities of a religious life. We can detect traces of possible dangers due to his spiritual unsophistication and the mistaken zeal of the other members of the Group in the matter of "Group Guidance," but he has now reached the point where he looks on such things from a more critical viewpoint. An interesting result of his change of attitude is his willingness to give time to philanthropy. Here we have an insight into the role that religion may play in the development of the philanthropic attitude.

George Linkman

George Linkman attended a Houseparty in 1923 when he was an undergraduate at an Eastern university. His family was not well off and his background was strongly religious. He was somewhat dissatisfied with his life—now he feels not enough so—and his interest was warm and appreciative though he was not "changed," for the idea of conversion had not been presented to him before nor did it occur to him at the Houseparty. He was never active in the Group, and is now a Presbyterian medical missionary.

He always kept certain reservations as to the genuineness of his experience, but nevertheless he feels it to have been beneficial in showing him "why I should be aggressive in Christian spiritual work." It increased his sense of religious certainty through making prayer more real, and it was beneficial to his moral and ethical habits, his capacity to deal with his personal problems, and his attitude toward sex. It had no harmful effects and was considered moderately emotional. He has not had sufficient contact with the movement lately to feel capable of judging it, but feels that movements of this general type are invaluable in reaching certain otherwise inaccessible people and in emphasizing such easily forgotten points as the universality of sin and the need for right relations to both God and man.

The benefits of Linkman's experience were probably limited by his reservations concerning its genuineness. However, these same reservations no doubt saved him from excesses that might have been harmful to him. As it was, it comprised a factor that he feels was beneficial in his spiritual development.

Ross Danforth

Ross Danforth was attending theological school in 1921 when he first came in contact with the Oxford Group. His religious background had been average and his family not well off. He was somewhat "but not abnormally" dissatisfied with his life and had already experienced conversion; however, the Group suggested to him his need for reconversion. His maximum interest was "psychological and personal," but he was never committed to the movement. He is now a Congregational minister in a New Jersey town.

Of his contact he says:

> My religious experience has been largely independent of the Oxford Group, but I have recognized valid and vital techniques for the discovery and development of personal religious experience in the movement. I have never been antagonistic but rather appreciative. Its influence has been beneficial to me because it has brought a challenge to seek reality in religious experience and has helped in overcoming self-deceptions. . . . Possibly it has enlarged my understanding of the personal religious life.

The experience increased his sense of religious certainty, the meaning of life, his zest for living, and his energies. It had no influence on his studies or his vocational choice, but otherwise it was beneficial. To his intellectual equipment it added an "interest in individual persons." The experience for him was only slightly emotional. He is now interested in and appreciative of the movement though not part of it. Some of his best friends are active leaders in it.

The most fundamental sources of Danforth's religious life were outside of the Oxford Group. However, it was a factor that challenged him, helped him to appraise himself more clearly, enhanced his religious vitality, and increased his interest in life. It might be questioned whether an "interest in individual persons" is an intellectual rather than a social or moral attitude; but at any rate he feels that emotion played but a slight part in his experience. One wonders why so appreciative an observer does not become active in the movement. Though he does not specify it, the answer obviously is that he has found his spiritual orientation outside of the Group so that he does not personally feel drawn to it.

Mrs. Ross Danforth

Mrs. Ross Danforth is the wife of the clergyman whose experience has been reviewed immediately above. She was attending a school of religious education in 1922 when she met Dr. Buchman. Her family was but nominally religious and was moderately well off. She had not been brought up to look for a conversion, nor was she dissatisfied with her life. It is interesting to know that she was one of the first women that Buchman tried to convert. The immediate result was a strong emotional upset, yet her interest in the Group was warm and appreciative, and for six years she was very active as a leader in the Group's work with girls.

Of her contact she says:

His [Buchman's] attempt to convince me of the error of my ways (which chiefly consisted in having gone tea-dancing at the Copley-Plaza during Christmas vacation) ended in nervous shock and illness for me and great disapproval and concern on the part of several professors. I might add two things: —Frank was not nearly so narrow as time went on and was infinitely thoughtful with most of us and truly kind—and I, in spite of the nervous upset, continued to be grateful to him and loyal for many years. In the three years spent at college it was Frank who gave me that which was most real and vital, and for which I had the deepest need. . . .

I feel the experiences to have been genuine although influenced by strong emotion. I think they had a direct relation to God and that the fellowship of the Group stimulated a growth that would have been more gradual and far less rich otherwise. It gave me a rigorous training in self-discipline, it gave entrance to a deeper Christian fellowship than I have ever found since, it gave color and glow and a sense of fine adventure to life.

In addition it increased her sense of religious certainty, the meaning of life, her zest for living, and her energies. It benefitted her social life in school and her capacity to deal with her own problems. Intellectually it trained her "to be more specific and honest with myself."

Her testimony with respect to the movement today is interesting and worth quoting at some length:

I feel I owe so much to what the Group gave me for six years that I hate to criticise or hear it criticised now. But I think it has gone through various phases and changed a good deal in the past twenty years, and I cannot be a part of it now.

The reasons for which I ceased to be an active member of the Group were several in number. I married one who was not an active member and yet whose religious life was as disciplined and as deep and whose whole attitude toward people was more, I felt, like that of Christ. We both felt and still do (1) that while we believed in the guidance of God, we could not go as far as those in the Group do. To me it seemed almost sacrilegious to carry the thought of "Guidance" into trivialities. (2) that there is a spiritual exclusiveness about the Group. If you do not use the Group technique and terminology, you are not authentically and wholly Christian. I think the women err in this direction more than do the men. (3) I don't know very much about the fairly recent trend toward "M.R.A." but a lot of it seems like rather cheap and superficial publicity. I think the original emphasis had much of infinite value in it, much of which I deeply wish we were more conscious of in the Christian Church.

It was the challenge and the deep fellowship of the Group that constituted its appeal for Mrs. Danforth, and raised her life, already committed to religious service, to a higher plane. Her opinion with respect to the Group of today is particularly interesting as coming from one palpably sincere and sensitive to its essential values, yet at the same time reluctantly forced to testify to what she considers its weak points. It is significant also that recognition of the Christian character of her husband's life, not centered in the Group, saved her from the narrowness of many members who see in it the only road to salvation.

But most interesting of all is the fact that Dr. Buchman's poor conversion technique resulted in a nervous upset. The fact that despite this Mrs. Danforth feels so appreciative of what he did for her testifies to a core of genuineness and soundness in his attitude and message. This case suggests that while psychiatrists who point to the dangers in the Group methods may indeed be right, yet there are religious values and compensations that often justify the risks. There is no doubt that in Mrs. Danforth's mind her unhappy emotional experience pales into insignificance compared with the Group's positive contribution to her personal development.

R. Austin Bailey

R. Austin Bailey's family was well-to-do with average religious interests. In 1925, at twenty-three, Bailey had graduated from an engineering school and was in business when he came in contact with the Group. He describes his interests as "appreciative but detached." As a result of his contact, particularly with one of the leaders, he went into the Episcopal ministry and now holds an important post in a Southern city.

He has always looked on his experience as genuinely religious. It increased his sense of religious certainty, the meaningfulness of life, and his energies. As already noted, it was the influence that changed his life work. It was in no way harmful. Of the Group at present he says, "It is a genuinely religious movement." He admires it and its leaders but says he never really "belonged."

Bailey is one of the abler of the younger ministers in his denomination. While the data on his questionnaire is scanty, the important thing that stands out is that the Group was the influence that turned him from engineering to the ministry. He is another example of the service of the Group to religion in turning able men to the ranks of the ministry.

George Muirhead

George Muirhead's family was in moderate circumstances and of average religious interests. He had graduated from an Eastern college and was in theological school in 1924, when, over a period of two years, he attended a number of House-parties and Oxford Group meetings. He had been dissatisfied with his life and had been "attracted but not wholeheartedly committed." He had not looked forward to a conversion, nor did his contact suggest it to him. This came later in a way that had no connection with the Group and involved a deepening of his allegiance to the Church. He is now an Episcopal clergyman.

Of the experience he says:

> It played a real part as preparation for later conversion experience. I always had a dim sense that the Buchmanite way was not normal or entirely right. The sense deepened in me and led me to seek for, to find, and to interpret the experience in a more peculiarly church, catholic way. But it did stress quiet time, spiritual earnestness, and at a time when my religion was almost entirely in the intellectual stages, kept before me the realization that true religion is *life,* not merely *ideas.*

Outside of this the experience had slight influence on him either beneficial or the reverse, though he does say that it aroused his curiosity about sex. It added nothing intellectual and was largely emotional.

He has the following to say of his present attitude toward the movement and its leaders:

> I respect them—but consider its methods (especially its way of prayer) open to question as too facile. I believe the Church should recognize their contribution as one especially needed in the Episcopalian church. I feel little if any attraction to commit myself to the movement today—mainly because I have found in the Church's life a feeding and spiritual life which to me seem more theologically grounded and fruitful.

For Muirhead the experience apparently supplied the emotional preparation for his fuller religious life in the church and the balance to his previous intellectual preoccupation with religion. Yet in no sense was the Oxford Group the center of his religious orientation, even temporarily. Here we see the Group playing a very useful but auxiliary part in the religious development of a clergyman.

The Positive Cases

Herbert Ives

Herbert Ives' family was in moderate circumstances and had average religious interests. When younger, some rather emotional religious experiences at a boys' camp had inclined him toward the ministry, which he eventually had chosen as his vocation. He had attended a well-known Eastern college and was studying abroad in 1927 when, at the age of thirty, he met several Group leaders at Oxford. At this time he was dissatisfied with his life in that he wanted to help people, especially those in trouble, and did not know how. In this respect the Group helped him greatly, and also gave him "a wholly new appreciation of the guidance of the Holy Spirit" as well as practical help in his personal life. His interest he describes as "very warm," and he was active in the Group for fourteen years. He is now a Presbyterian clergyman in upper New York State.

He feels his experiences with the Group to have been genuinely religious and "guidance" to have been explainable only by reference to God. The influence of the experience was on the whole beneficial:

> Until recently, my contact with the Group, like my earlier decision to enter the ministry, brought me face to face with God and the claims of the New Testament. It made my religion personal and practical, and an experience to give to others.

It increased his sense of religious certainty, the meaningfulness of life, and his energies; also, until recently, his zest for living. With respect to his attitude toward life he says, "I believe my own faith in God's presence and love and power to have been immeasurably deepened." His church attendance, fairly regular before his contact, became not so regular; but now, after withdrawing from Moral Re-Armament, it has become much more regular. It was definitely beneficial to his moral and ethical habits, and also to his capacity for dealing with his personal problems "mainly through increased honesty, deeper fellowship and regular prayer." It helped his attitude toward sex through greater realism, openness, and a sense of forgiveness for sin.

In other ways the influence was more complicated. With respect to his social life he feels the experience reduced his self-consciousness but made him somewhat officious. While it gave him a message as a minister, it limited his contribution to the Church; and it narrowed his interests. Intellectually, he says, "It helped me to see the practical implications of the fundamentals of Christianity—enlarged my whole conception of prayer, forgiveness, etc." Emotion was only slightly present —not nearly so much so as in his earlier experiences. As a result of the newer experience he became convinced that the religious life involves both gradual growth and crises, such as conversion, often repeated.

Since he has been quite close to many leaders in the Group his comments are significant as well as interesting:

Recent years have brought conflict between some of the Group leadership and my own deepest convictions. Domination on the part of some individuals tended to force many of us into forced, stereotyped activity. The very rapid growth of the early years was replaced by more limited stereotyped activity in recent years, as e.g. all planning in the U.S.A. was done by a comparatively small "team." I feel the work in America at least has recently become a kind of "closed corporation"—almost a new denomination—preoccupied with one, limited form of action and no longer interested, primarily, in re-kindling the Church.

Whenever, as abroad, Frank [Buchman] has been "successful" the tone of the work has become co-operative and friendly. In this country, especially, where he has faced so much criticism, the work has tended more and more to be self-conscious, defensive, and smug.

I still feel a re-alignment with and in the Church would be healthy and fortunate for both the Group and the Protestant church.

Ives' analysis of his experience is particularly full and discriminating. His fundamental interest in his ministry lay in people, and his desire to help them seems to have been largely frustrated before his contact with the Group. Here was offered him the technique and power to deal with people as well as help for his personal problems, all of which was necessary to make his ministry effective. Hence the Group met the deep needs of his nature, and this explains his fourteen years of work with the movement. It is interesting to note that emotion played a slight part in his experience, especially as compared with his earlier religious crisis. This is no doubt an example of a phenomenon noticed by other investigators; namely, that the emotional element in religious experiences tends to decrease with age.

GARDNER NEWHALL

Gardner Newhall's family was well-off, cultivated, and had average religious interests. His religious training was of a rather conventional Congregationalist type, which instilled in him the usual dogmas and attitudes of the denomination, and did not lead him to expect conversion. By the time he entered an Eastern university he was filled with guilt feelings, chiefly over sex, which resulted in a lack of purpose and a disintegration of personality which, in turn, seriously interfered with his college life and studies. At this time, in 1926, he fell in with the Group. He was not "changed," though one of the leaders gave him much attention, but he describes his interest as "very warm and appreciative," and he was active for about one year. He is now a psychiatric physician.

He felt the experience genuinely religious and still does, though he interpreted it in psychological terms. Of it he says:

I still feel the same. I never experienced "Guidance" in quite the same way as some, because of my belief that it was a special psychological reaction to a constantly renewed determination to do what was "good." I believed (believe) that this emotional reaction is of importance—i.e. harmony can only be obtained in that way.

Its influence was beneficial. It freed me from conflicts between good and bad by (1) redefining my concept of bad so that sex ceased to be a moral issue and became a practical one; (2) by giving me a feeling for the reality of goodness and the practical worth of striving for it. . . .

It changed my attitude toward life in a definitely constructive way. It was a real "experience" and convinced me (1) that our concept of sin has got to be more realistically social and psychological, and (2) of the value of "high ideals."

The experience increased his sense of religious certainty, the meaning of life, his zest for living, and his energies. Except for hobbies and interests, on which it had no effect, all items on the check list are marked as being benefitted, particularly studies and social life in college. It "aroused my curiosity as to how the mind works." Morally and ethically "it enabled me to live a freer and healthier life, especially sexually, and gave me a sense of the value of my fellow man." He gave up his habit of church-going, which had been more or less forced on him before the experience; but he says that this change may not have been the result of the experience. It added to his intellectual equipment "only by freeing me from conflicts so that I became free to think," and was largely emotional and due, he feels, to the sense of freedom and release. He further analyses its effect on him as follows:

I feel that the benefit I derived from the "houseparties" was largely due to a crystallization of my life purposes. Though those purposes were vague, I fully sensed their direction. It gave meaning to my college work. An equally important result of the "houseparties" was an almost complete removal of considerable guilt over sex. I came to realize that sex itself was a normal and healthy part of life. I realized then that in itself it was healthy; that it is a "sin" only when it is used to hurt someone. And further, I saw that the concept of right and wrong is purely a relative one; also that one has to interpret social codes as intelligently as possible.

To sum this up: The "houseparties" enabled me to find an intelligent solution of the universal conflict between the sex instincts and social codes—the conflict that besets all adolescents.

He sums up his present attitude toward the movement as

favorable, though I now know little about it. I believe, however, that in many individuals it tends to increase their guilt sense rather than the reverse. This would be harmful.

This testimony is particularly interesting as coming from a psychiatrist whose training is evident in his analysis of the experience; also in the psychological tone of his explanations as compared with the more theistic approach of most of the others. He says,

Within my psychological definition of religion, I believe that all religious phenomena can be explained potentially by psychological findings and theories.

It is interesting to note that it seems to have been the experience itself which caused him to be less theological and moral, and more psychological in his approach to life. Sex "ceased to be a moral issue," and he became more curious about the mind. That this was possible is an indication of the dogmatic freedom allowed in the early days of the Group —the "experience" was what was emphasized, and this was a very real factor in Newhall's life, being an influence that was integrating, releasing, energizing, and permanent in its beneficial effects.

As a psychiatrist with Freudian training, Dr. Newhall is much more aware of the part sex played in his experience, and hence his answers constitute a very searching and valuable document. This is also true of Robert Elser, who, significantly, had been psychoanalyzed. These two cases, therefore, give us insights into what probably was an important factor in many of the cases where, through lack of trained understanding or perhaps reticence, it has been glossed over. Also this case is an interesting contrast to many others where very similar experiences are described in theological rather than psychological terms.

In summary we may say that here we have an example of a young man to whom the Group ministered by meeting his need for freedom from guilt feelings that were preventing him from arriving at a rational solution of the sexual anxieties which were causing uncertainty and disintegration. At the same time his idealism was given meaning, and his interests were oriented in a more social, unselfish direction.

Chapter Seventeen

The Positive Active Cases

Margaret Anderson

Margaret Anderson's background was strongly religious. She had been graduated from a finishing school for girls and then had married. At the age of twenty-six she says she was dissatisfied with herself in being "filled with fear, and was also difficult to get along with." Though a regular church-goer, she had not been brought up to expect conversion; but in 1928 she came in contact with the Group through a relative, and as a result of this and reading such authors as Begbie, James, and Shoemaker, she was "changed." Ever since then she has been active in the movement, giving full time to it, and is now "in active touch with all concerned both in America and Britain." She is an Episcopalian.

Naturally the experience appealed to her as genuinely religious at the time. Of it she says:

My feeling is *absolutely* the same *now*. Different persons, different methods may help bring one to a spiritual experience and knowledge of the guidance of God—but it is not a thing you "see through." You either *know* it or haven't yet experienced it.

The influence of the experience was most certainly beneficial by giving new power and purpose to my life—through bringing me into contact with the *Reality* of God. It changed my attitude toward life very definitely in a constructive, creative way—has given me something to live for, a concrete goal to work for; i.e., a better world under God's control and helping to meet the needs of others. . . . Church services took on new meaning and most especially the Sacraments.

The experience increased her religious certainty, the meaning of life, her zest for living, and her energies. It stimulated her to study, and she assumed her home responsibilities more effectively. It improved moral and ethical habits, broadened her interests, was of the greatest help in giving her the capacity to deal with her personal problems, and improved her attitude toward sex. There were no harmful effects. It added to her intellectual equipment "a sense of personal, national, and world responsibility" and "disciplined thought and efficiency." Of emotion she says, "There is always some beneficial emotion and release in a *genuine experience*. But it is the Will that makes it continual and permanent." As an active worker in the movement she naturally approves of it.

The testimony of Mrs. Anderson suggests a woman who before her experience had been a somewhat self-centered, perhaps slightly neurasthenic young society matron living a rather pointless existence. A religious upbringing may have added restlessness through the realization that her religious duty was not being done. For these dissatisfactions the Group supplied an antidote through the conversion experience and her subsequent work with the movement, which has been the point of orientation for her personality. The present fullness of her satisfaction with results is indicated by the absence of critical comments with respect to her own experience or the movement. Nevertheless it is interesting that she is the only respondent who makes a distinction between the emotions and the Will. But it is questionable whether a sense of "personal, national, and world responsibility" should be classed as an intellectual element rather than an emotional attitude. Mrs. Anderson's interest has lasted fourteen years; it has integrated her personality, given her a purpose, and made life seem worthwhile. She is an example of the Group's effectiveness in reaching the upper classes.

Lewis Dorrance

Lewis Dorrance was twenty-three and at theological school when he first became interested in the Group in 1927. His family was in moderate circumstances and strongly religious, though he had not been brought up to expect conversion. At the time he was "divided in mind as to values, future, etc.," and as a result of personal conversations with men in the Group he was "changed." He is the Rector of an Episcopal church in a Southern state and is still active in the Group.

He says of the experience and its effects:

> I feel the experience to have been genuine religious conversion, followed by true guidance. It clarified my vision—made me sure of my vocation—gave me a power to resist temptation—enlisted all my best thinking and work—showed me what the country and world need and how to begin to meet that need. It made me more optimistic, surer that God is working His purpose out.

The experience was beneficial in every way suggested by the questionnaire and in no way harmful. Intellectually it gave him "particularly the habit of looking for the Holy Spirit's light on my own mental processes." It was moderately emotional. He believes in the movement completely.

This is another illustration of integration of personality and consequent power through experience with the Oxford Group.

The Oxford Group

The Reverend Henry Sampson

The Reverend Henry Hart Sampson is a prominent Episcopalian clergyman, retired. He attended a Middle Western college where he acquired several degrees and has been in touch with educational institutions throughout his career. In 1932, at the age of fifty-nine, he attended a Houseparty in California for the sake of observing the Group's methods. As an Episcopalian he had never expected a conversion and was not particularly dissatisfied with his life. "I thought I was pretty good until I found out all the things that were wrong with me." His interest he describes as first merely curious, then appreciative, and finally "changed." He then decided to give his full time to the movement and has been working with the Group ever since, being particularly interested and successful in work with students and with alcoholics.

Of his experience he says:

It was a spiritual awakening uncovering new power, new joy, new certainty; a scientific demonstration of how spiritual laws work when accurately applied. Guidance is definite direction by God in the affairs of daily life. It has its laws governing it, which must be accurately observed. The experience was beneficial in that it improved my health by getting rid of my resentments. . . . It has enlarged my sympathies, broadened my interest in people and their problems, and has helped me to help alcoholics become high-ranking officers in the Army, Navy, and leaders in business. It has brought together broken families, including my own, when all other means had failed. . . . Being honest is the most revolutionary experience in life. No one who has never tried it can imagine the sense of release that comes with being absolutely honest with yourself and someone you can trust. This with your surrender of your whole self to God is the greatest experience in life. Try it and see! This constitutes the laboratory test, the only real scientific test —there is no real knowledge otherwise.

The experience was in no way harmful to him. Intellectually it gave him new flexibility:

> It got me out of the narrow, prejudiced grooves that curse the average so-called "intellectual." Helped me to be tolerant of intolerant people and opened a new world of people and ideas.

With respect to emotion he says:

> I do not think that emotion played a part at first. I was critical and had to be convinced step by step. It was first a coldly intellectual search. When I finally tried it, I got a new sense of power, release, and a deep sense of inner peace and happiness as the result.

Although he holds certain reservations concerning Moral Re-Armament, he is very enthusiastic about the Group's work, its techniques, accomplishments, and possibilities. He finds its value demonstrated empirically:

> It demonstrates its worth like everything else, by its results. If you try it out on your problems you find it works. That is the answer. . . . I have worked with hundreds of High School and College students and have never detected any harmful effects when the laws laid down were obeyed. . . . As a working philosophy for life under all conditions, and all ages it is the most scientific, effective plan I have discovered after forty years of research. . . . We have sent hundreds back to their Church because they wanted to go after getting fear, frustration, criticism, and hatred out of their lives. These include Roman Catholics, Protestants, Christian Scientists, Mormons, and Jews. Having found God as a reality, they wished to worship Him. With our young people . . . it has made them more altruistic in their vocational choices . . . fostered a higher standard of moral and ethical habits, had a wholsesome effect on their hobbies and interests, and provided a daily check on their personal problems on the basis of honesty, purity, unsel-

fishness and love. Facing sex on this basis offers the only fearless and effective solution to this sex problem, the major problem of life.

Dr. Sampson does not specify very clearly just what he considers the laws of the method or how he has observed them to have been disobeyed, but he has specified many ways in which he has seen them do good.

With respect to his own experience, his interest in the movement had its origin in an intellectual curiosity which gradually took on emotional warmth as he saw its results on others and began to become involved himself. Its beneficial effect on his home life suggests that it met basic personal needs. However, it seems to be its effect on others that best explains the Group's hold on him. Since he has spent a lifetime in searching for such a power no doubt its success moves him the more. In this sense his interest is more objective than with most of the other respondents. His depth of conviction is manifest through the evangelical note that is evident in his testimony. His case is further unusual in this study not only in that he was older than the average when he became interested in the Group, but his approach was, at least at the beginning, much more intellectual. This is another illustration of the theory that conversion in later life is more apt to involve cognitive elements.

Chapter Eighteen

A Commentary on the Cases

The reader who has plowed through all the varying stories of experiences with the Group may feel a little bewildered as to what conclusions to draw. This chapter will contain some informal observations summarizing the information to be gleaned from the case histories and pointing out certain implications.

The first and most obvious observation is that few of our respondents have maintained their active connection with the Group for a very long period. Even if we include five persons who responded by letter to the effect that they could not describe their experience, four of whom would have fallen in the Positive Active category, we would still have not many more than one in ten who had remained with the Group permanently. Of course these represent a past generation of Group supporters and things may have changed, but the impression that one gets is that the loyalty of present-day supporters is even more ephemeral. There are a few names that one still finds celebrated in the *New World News* that appeared in its early issues of five years before, but a great many world figures who were represented as hailing M.R.A. as the hope of civilization have disappeared from its pages. Whether the ideals of the Group are too high and demanding, or whether it has subtle shortcomings, as suggested in some of our case histories, there seems little doubt but that complete loyalty to the Group and its program tends to be a short-range rather than a long-range affair.

On the other hand, a second feature of our data, almost equally apparent, is that the great majority have felt their contact to have been beneficial rather than harmful. Many have looked on their experience as the turning point and focus of their moral and spiritual lives. Only eleven of our fifty-five respondents, or one in five, felt the experience harmful, and of these only one seems to have felt that the harm was far-reaching and lasting. One nervous upset was ascribed to the manipulations of Dr. Buchman, but this respondent in retrospect indicated that values received far outweighed the harm. In still another case the Group failed to benefit a neurotic condition which was afterward successfully treated by psychoanalysis. The Group and its methods have often been cited as a menace to mental health. Taken as a whole, our population of fifty-five does not exhibit any more harmful results than we might expect from any movement vital enough to affect the emotions of its followers. Furthermore these harmful results are more than counterbalanced by the good that has been done. The fact that so many of those who report benefits are now critical of the movement gives one added confidence in the positive aspects of their personal testimony.

When we try to explain why the Group was beneficial to some and harmful to others, we must confess that this is largely bound up with complexities of the individual personality with which we could not deal. However, one does note a tendency for the Negative cases to be those who were actively interested for only a short time, while those who have the best things to say of the values they received tend to be those who were active in the movement for at least a year. There are a few exceptions to this generalization; nevertheless this observation suggests that the emotional upheaval accompanying "change" was not enough to complete the experience unless the changed attitudes were in some way practiced. However, once these attitudes were stamped in and made permanent the individual might leave the movement, as most did, with considerable assurance that the new values would have lasting worth. This observation would coincide with psychological laws, and particularly in cases where he was particularly interested in a convert's allegiance, Buchman showed himself a master of practical psychology in providing the individual with many opportunities to practice his new-found convictions.

Perhaps the most dangerous aspect of Group experience is a too naïve reliance on "guidance" coupled with the encouragement of the untrained to interfere with intimate personal affairs. An example of this is suggested in the case of Susan Robertson, who through guidance conceived a mistaken idea and was saved from taking a very serious step through the personal help of a non-Groupist clergyman. However, the recent emphases on "checking" guidance and group guidance, though perhaps objectionable from certain points of view, nevertheless tend to mitigate this danger about which we have been speaking.

Another aspect of our cases that we notice is that many turned toward religion or other altruistic work as the result of their contact with the Group. Of course a certain number were already committed to religion, while still others would very likely have come to it if left to themselves anyway. There is perhaps the suggestion here and there that the Group tended to force others into religious work when it would have been unnatural for them; but on the whole it would seem that the Group has had a wholesome effect on younger people so that religious work, the teaching profession, and other altruistic vocations have been enriched by the incursion of many an able and vital personality who otherwise might be contributing less valuably to society in more materialistic lines of endeavor.

It will be noted that our respondents tend to come from families in the upper-income levels. This was perhaps inevitable from the fact that most of our population were attending college or seminary at the time, but it has been noted that Buchman specialized in those colleges where wealth and social prestige would be found. Over half of the individuals came from families with incomes over $5,000, while well over a fourth represented families with more than $10,000. Another confirmation of the general impression that the Group is a movement of the middle and upper classes is found in the religious denominations represented, where nearly nine out ten are affiliated with either the Episcopal, Congregational, or Presbyterian churches. This is despite the fact that the Group type of evangelism has always been more indigenous to churches such as the Baptist and Methodist, while Buchman's connections might have been expected to be with Lutherans or members of pietistic sects.

It will be noticed also that about half of the respondents come from families that are strongly religious, while none come from completely non-religious homes. Also there was some tendency for the Positive cases to come from more religious homes. This supports what psychologists have demonstrated, that few individuals, if any, are converted to religious belief in later life who had not received some religious instruction in childhood or youth. This suggests that the Oxford Group does not wholly "change" people so much as it builds on foundations already laid, supplying emotional power to put into practice ideals long accepted. The conversion is emotional and volitional rather than intellectual.

Along with the emotional stimulus of the experience there usually went, particularly for the Positive cases, an increase in religious certainty, sense of the meaning of life, and vital energies. It has been often said and sometimes demonstrated that a religious environment is favorable to accomplishment. Many of our cases show how this can be so. The added meaning which a fresh religious vision gives to a person, increasing his sense of the importance of the universe as well as that of his own place in it, stimulates not only his interest in life but his energies, so that whatever he sets out to do is more effectively accomplished than before.

Consequently it is not surprising to find that many report benefit to their moral habits and their ethics. But it is interesting to note that some of the same people who testified to improvement in their own ethics yet criticised the ethics of the movement as a whole. It appears that we have here a familiar instance where the ethics of individuals are superior to the movement or the institution of which they form a part and which may even be the means of nourishing those ethics. This hints that the Oxford Group in a certain paradoxical way may be good for individuals at the same time that it may be doing harm to the social structure, as when Buchman lauded Hitler as a Christian bulwark. It is of further significance that many stated that the Group had helped their capacity to deal with their own problems, especially since a criticism of the Group often heard is its destructive and disintegrating effect on personality. Only four of our fifty-five seemed to lend much support to this criticism.

On the other hand, there were many who felt the movement had adversely affected their attitude toward sex, though even here the majority of those who replied to this item indicated that the effect had been beneficial. As is to be expected, most of the Negative cases were to be found with the first category, while Positive cases made up the great majority of the latter. In other words, there was a strong tendency for a favorable experience with the Group as a whole to be linked with a healthy reaction toward its approach to sex. This evidence is interesting, for the Group probably will never quite live down the charges of its critics that it has in the past been guilty of over-featuring the subject of sex. It will be recalled that this was the main contention of its opponents at Princeton. Regardless of the fact that there was probably considerably more smoke than there was fire, we can sense at least some justification for the charges. Even in his days at Penn State, Buchman had the reputation of being absorbedly interested in converting sexual sinners. Indeed, among a certain element of the student body it was said that the best way for a student to enlist his sympathy and help was to go to him and confess a sexual sin. Undoubtedly, in banking too heavily on this road as a means of convicting almost anyone of sin, he often overreached himself. It is true that with many young people there was great need for them to bring their sexual conflicts into the open, and we have commented on his skill in dealing with this topic in many situations. But doubtless with some the effect was only to increase tensions rather than alleviate them, and these are the people to whom the Group's handling of sexual topics did more harm than it did good. Without doubt, the sad experience of the Group with hostility aroused by this touchy subject had much to do with its present policy of de-emphasizing sex. No longer is it the practice to deal with it in open gatherings, but the Group still has to contend with the echoes of ghosts which, having once been raised, are now hard to lay.

Those who attend Group functions often hear the comment that there is nothing emotional about the experience, but on the contrary that the Group's chief stock in trade is ideas.

"Ideas Have Legs," is the title of a recent Group best-seller by the English journalist Peter Howard. In this iteration the Group strikes the shrewd observer as protesting too much. Since the critics of the Group maintain a position that is exactly the opposite, one of the aims of the questionnaire was to discover what participants thought about it. They provide us with much more evidence of emotional than intellectual content, and it would seem pretty clear from what we know of Dr. Buchman, the quality of most of the Group literature, and what goes on at a typical Group gathering that it is not intellectual elements that monopolize the foreground.

This is not to say, however, that the large part that emotion plays in Group procedures is necessarily an improper one. Since emotion is not quite respectable in the circles where the Group makes its appeal, its publicity responds to a sound advertising instinct in de-emphasizing the mechanics of its work with personality in this regard. As a matter of fact, many of our respondents recognized that while the part played by emotion was large, nevertheless it was healthy. This was not always so, particularly for the Negative cases, who felt their experiences to have been emotional and harmful, but the Group's chief contribution to personal integration was not so much new ideas as a change in attitude. Along with the change in attitude went the emotional energy necessary to put the attitude into practice.

The question immediately arises whether the Group's intellectual poverty, taken in conjunction with the emotion reported to be present, does not suggest a very dangerous situation. It has already been maintained that this neglect of the mind is the chief weakness of the Group, which explains many of its mistakes and failures. On the other hand, this study shows that its mistakes, at least in its personal work, have not been nearly as serious as one might expect; for the case histories in this study are concrete evidence of a very considerable measure of success in the chief aspect of the Group's work, personal evangelism. The answer is doubtless to be found in the religious background of the participants in the Group experience. For the most part, they already had absorbed religious thinking and teaching. Their weakness was not so much that they did not know about religion but that they had accepted it without living it. They needed not so much ideas, for the time being, but emotional energy to put into practice those which they had. Consequently this reservoir of Christian teaching guided the average member in his behavior on the one hand, while on the other it formed the intellectual center for the integration that the emotional drives of the Group made possible. If we see the Group as mainly concerned with the emotions and the will rather than as a storehouse of theology and ideas, we will come much closer to understanding its true function with personality.

It is worth noting briefly what factors led to the experience. It will be noticed that most of the respondents report being dissatisfied with themselves before the experience. Theologically this is what is meant by "conviction of sin," though very few of the respondents actually used this term. This was partly the raw material out of which the Group fashioned conversions, while partly this conviction was deliberately fostered by Buchman and his disciples in order to effect conversions. Trivial faults would do for this if more heinous matter were not available, as in the case of the Hartford Seminary student whose habits were so impeccable that Buchman had to convict him of sin on the basis of petty extravagance, or in the case of Mrs. Ross Danforth whose sin was attending a tea-dance. Another important factor was supplied by the Group in its suggesting by personal contact, public testimony, its literature, and other means, that conversion was possible. Dr. Buchman is a master in the use of suggestion, and a tribute to his skill in this way is the fact that so many of our respondents had never before thought of conversion in connection with themselves while some had not even known that such a thing was possible.

The attitudes of these participants toward the movement is not the least interesting aspect of their responses. Here a clear distinction must be made between the respondents' appraisals of their own experiences and their attitudes toward the movement. Although all of those whose personal experience was negative had a corresponding attitude toward the movement, this correlation did not hold for those in the Positive groups, one of whose members looks on the movement as a "lure of the devil." Only the three members of the Positive Active group approved of the movement without reservation, and even one of those is critical of M.R.A. In general we may say that there was considerably more criticism of the Group than there was approval. Among the criticisms most frequently expressed were the following: (a) that there is too much interest in the rich for a Christian fellowship, (b) that the Group violates its own standard of absolute honesty, particularly in its publicity, (c) that it is becoming a religious dictatorship, (d) that members are too ready to meddle in complicated personal problems that they do not understand, (e) that it is blind to social evil, and by its complacency is helping to perpetuate the shortcomings of the present social order, (f) that its conception of "guidance" is naïve and often dangerous, (g) that its theology is childish and inadequate. These criticisms help to explain why so many left the Group.

Frequent appreciations were that it (a) affords a deep experience of fellowship; (b) challenges the individual to express the best that is in him; (c) has vitalized from without the religious life of the churches; (d) has given power to individuals to live more effectively, often turning defeat and frustration into victorious living; (e) has opened the eyes of many to spiritual reality.

Respondents differed widely in their opinions of Dr. Buchman, ranging from those who look on him as a charlatan to those who see him as a devoted servant of the Lord. However, there was no criticism of his essential sincerity voiced by anyone who had ever known him intimately despite protracted efforts to locate such criticism.

PART IV

Explanation and Appraisal

Chapter Nineteen

Why Does the Group Appeal?

"WHAT DO YOU know of the Oxford Group?" "What do you think of the Oxford Group?" These are the twin questions one is most apt to hear whenever the topic of the Group comes to the front. The first of these questions has been dealt with in the foregoing pages of our book. It remains for us to direct ourselves to the second.

It is not that any final evaluation can be made of a movement whose story is not yet finished and which in any case is too complex for conclusions with which no one could quarrel. But as a movement on the contemporary scene, the Oxford Group raises issues about our society that are larger than itself. A commentary on the Oxford Group is a commentary on our world, our country, our religion, and ourselves. Has it the answer to our world-sickness? Can it supply the new spirit which will allay our national frictions and solve our social problems? Can it revive our worn-out and tired churches? Can we trust it with a sure hand, to minister to the soul-hunger of the average individual, who longs for salvation? These are the questions to which the Group has positive and ready answers. A consideration of ourselves and the world in which we live will at least suggest some of the reasons why the Group has succeeded where other agencies have failed. But it will help us to understand some of its weaknesses as well.

The human psyche is like the human stomach in at least

this one respect, namely, that it is the seat of hungers that deprivation makes only the more poignant. The average person, however, is only dimly aware of exactly what his psychological hungers are and how they can best be satisfied. But the Oxford Group, with that keen practical knowledge of human souls which it owes to its founder, has not only diagnosed some of mankind's deepest hungers but offers the satisfaction for them. It is not that from time immemorial the great religions have not also recognized these hungers and from time to time have satisfied them, but the Group at present is providing many with the substance where their churches in many instances are offering them merely shadows.

Of all these hungers perhaps the most far-reaching is the longing for goodness and purity. Negatively speaking, this is the sense of guilt, which each of us carries around with us in some form. Certain psychologists may cry out against it, saying that it, along with evil, should be abolished. Nevertheless it remains, and though the psychiatrist at the consulting couch finds that it works much havoc with the neurotic personality, yet it is doubtful whether very much of the world's most important work could be accomplished were it not for the peculiarly human capacity to feel uncomfortable when accomplishment falls short of aim. Both the psychiatrist and the Group want to reduce this sense of guilt—the former by reducing aim, the latter by increasing the accomplishment.

The typical individual touched by the Group brings to it a sensitive conscience and Christian ideals, the fruit of a religious upbringing. As in the case of many a Christian, he is troubled by numerous conflicts due to the large gap existing between his profession and his performance. He knows what he *ought* to do and yet he doesn't do it. Furthermore, these tensions are bottled up within him to an extent of which he himself is unaware. The Group not only opens a safety valve in the form of confession but somehow supplies him with the energy and capacity for the first time to make actual that ideal of conduct for himself which from childhood he has always cherished. Part of the process of getting rid of guilt feelings involves the discovery that many others are in the same boat. One of the results of confession is the discovery that others have been or are bedeviled by the same conflicts or problems. Buchman makes much of the joys of a "fellowship of sinners," which is an important element in the phenomenon of which we speak. The whole experience results in a sense of relief and freedom the savor of which is so delightful that only those who have experienced it can fully conceive of its relish.

This is particularly true of guilt feelings involving conflicts over sex, which we have seen has held such a prominent place in the Group's past history. While there is always the danger that the Group's methods may encourage an unhealthy emphasis on sexual sins and so increase guilt feelings, nevertheless, as our investigation has suggested, many secured a release from sexual anxieties through confession and through listening to the confessions of other "sinners" with the same problems. Particularly in the case of young people, this tended to save them from the sense of being social outcasts because of their guilt. Fairly typical was the case of Gardner Newhall, afterward a psychiatrist, who testifies that the experience was "an almost complete removal of considerable guilt over sex," and who as a result came to realize that sex itself is a "normal and healthy part of life."

Closely allied to the desire for ethical perfection is the longing for religious reality and the urge to do something active about it. Many Groupists, previous to their contact, felt a desire for a transforming spiritual experience which would somehow give genuineness and meaning to a faith merely professed by the lips and practiced, if at all, only in church-going. Sometimes this desire was an acute longing, as in the case of Susan Robertson, while in others it was present, if at all, only subconsciously. William Stuyvesant's life was relatively smooth and serene previous to his contact with the Group. But to many differing types the Group made God seem real and near, while through this sense of reality there flowed the power to live meaningful religious lives which produced, in the words of William James, "regenerative effects unattainable in other ways".

More generalized but allied with this hunger for an increasing sense of religious reality is the need for a livelier sense of all non-material value. Whether through his church, college course in English literature, or some other source, the average person of the type to which the Group makes its appeal knows that a materialistic civilization is weak and that the materialist's life is ultimately meaningless. Though he seldom thinks of himself as a materialist, yet his life is a hectic pursuit of materialistic symbols such as motor cars, rich acquaintances, club-memberships, and money. The Group itself is not without its weakness for such rewards of the world, yet in a kind of paradoxical way it does introduce its supporters to non-material values; for some this vision is a mere illusion, for others only a glimpse, but to a not inconsiderable number it is an experience of genuine spiritual reality.

Moreover, it is not only the gross materialists to whom the Group offers the refreshing waters of a spiritual life but the scientists and rationalists as well. This type of person is not drawn to the Group in as large numbers as the others because its program is not such as to attract the average rationalistic mind, yet an occasional student is attracted to the Group because of the philosophic aridity of his scientific or rationalistic studies. Indeed it is questionable whether our colleges and universities are not in process of killing the vitality of the culture which they supposedly serve by too great an emphasis on science and rationalization and too great neglect of the values of faith and religion. For this emphasis in our civilization the Group has been in some measure an antidote, and the actual effect on several of our respondents, such as Nathaniel Fielding and Samuel Smith, was to heighten the appreciation for the wider spiritual values.

With respect to these hungers of which we have been speaking, the desire for moral perfection and the longing for spiritual reality, it may be worth our while to pause and note that they are factors relatively unnoticed in the psychological pictures of the modern individual. Realistic novelists underestimate them, psychologists' attentions are directed to other things, while the cynic denies they exist. Yet Buchman's teacher, Henry Drummond, declared that the amount of spiritual longing in the world was absolutely incredible. Other spiritual-minded people have divined the same thing. Psychologically this was what Augustine meant when he prayed, "Our hearts are restless until they find their rest in Thee"; while it was Jesus Himself who spoke of those who hunger and thirst after righteousness. Just as the musician longs for his instrument and the artist for his brush, so there are uncounted thousands in our own day, as in ancient times, whose desire to make out of their own lives something that is pure, lovely, and of good report amounts almost to a passion. But yet this passion has become overlaid and frustrated. The simple and compelling accents of King James' English has at some time awakened the desire in the heart of nearly every youth who has read the story of the Gospels, but too often has its message been prostituted through inter-denominational bickerings, or turned aside by crusty dogma, lost in hollow ritualism or defeated by a one-day-a-week pharasaical brand of Christian respectability. Buchman and his Group have sensed this fertile field of spiritual longing, some of it actively struggling, some of it gone to sleep but nevertheless ready to be awakened. It is only by postulating its existence that we can make the success of the Oxford Group credible. For evidence of its reality one needs only to recall the testimony of many of the individuals whose histories we have chronicled in the previous section.

But though these are the hungers that psychologically are the most prominent among those which the Group attempts to satisfy, nevertheless there are others that must not be neglected.

Of these the craving for fellowship, group security, and status was an urge that many mentioned as being met to a deeply satisfying degree in the fellowship of the Group. It may be questioned why in the world of the present day, so well supplied with clubs and organizations and the apparatus of communication and friendship, another organization for the same purpose would have any outstanding appeal. The obvious answer is a commentary on our society. While we have made great progress in the forms of friendship and the verbalisms of brotherly love, we have not gone nearly so far with the reality. Most of us are satisfied with a very little in the way of friendship, and the sharing of a neighbor's views on the political situation, contacts at the bridge table, in the office, or over a cocktail glass; or at best, a job together on a church or community project, is what passes for friendship in the minds of many. The divorce rate is a tragic indication of how often true fellowship is unattained even within families. Just as there are many individuals with spiritual hungers unsatisfied, so there are even greater numbers whose spirits inwardly cry out to be known not for the façade which they erect for social and business purposes but for that which in their hearts they really believe themselves to be. Our Anglo-Saxon and Nordic cultures—and significantly it has been within these that the Group has enjoyed its greatest triumphs—do not encourage one to wear his heart on his sleeve, and part of the northerner's coldness lies in his lack of any skill or opportunity to exchange with others his most intimate concerns, his triumphs and his failures, his hopes and his fears; nor do what contacts he does allow himself very often involve anything much nobler than the pursuit of money or the search for social prestige. The Group, on the other hand, and without the benefit of liquor, ministers to men and women starving for fellowship on this thin fare, and many who have left the Group still look back on their association with it as an experience in fellowship the intensity of which they never felt before and have never enjoyed since. Such a reaction is illustrated by the case of Mrs. Ross Danforth, while even some of those otherwise negatively affected, like Robert Elser, sometimes recognized this quality in the movement. A member of a religious order, who might be expected to know something of the satisfaction of religious fellowship, told us that even though he had outgrown the Group he had yet to find its equal in the experience of intense and deeply satisfying friendship. Of course this level is not attained by everyone in the Group, since many simply enjoy being noticed by other people, for Groupists practice an almost professional friendliness; yet at its best the experience comes close to what is the ultimate in fellowship, namely the pursuit of the highest thing one knows, with one's most intimate thoughts normally and naturally an open book to others who share the same aims and confidences.

Carlyle says, "A person . . . is ever holy to us; a certain orthodox Anthropomorphism connects my *Me* with all other *Thees* in bonds of Love." The Group caters to this concern about other people, to like them and to be liked by them, which is never wholly absent from the relations of any two people and which especially characterizes the most satisfying relations between them. Many of our respondents testified to the fact that the Group had not only given them the power to help others, which had been lacking before, but also supplied them with the proper practical techniques. In other words, the Group satisfies the universal craving of people to work with their friends, to express love for and receive love from others, and to be known as they really are.

Participants find that the Group supplies another need, that for relaxation and quiet. The high pressure of modern life, the hectic whirl of activity into which one must plunge himself if he is to get credit for being successful, the appointments, the committees, the clubs and societies, with all the other myriad claims on a person's energies give little opportunity, as one respondent puts it, for the "quiet thinking through of problems." The Group is an activist movement devoted to doing things, not to thought. Yet its Quiet Time does supply a spiritual and mental relaxation which those who practice it find helpful in acquiring perspective, balance, and insight into the problems of life. Goethe and Emerson both teach us that action must alternate with thought, while Toynbee speaks of the values of Withdrawal and Return. The Group could learn from these three thinkers something of the meaning of real thought. Nevertheless, in its own way it does demonstrate this rhythm of alternation, and especially the lesson of the importance to the human spirit of periods of quiet and communion is one that needs learning in our day and age. The Group not only teaches it verbally but demonstrates it in action. This also helps to explain the appeal that it has for many persons.

Still another universal need is that for integration and orientation of the personality. Happy is the man or woman who so clearly sees what he needs or knows what he wants that no interfering urges or desires disturb him in the pursuit of what for him is the highest value. Of such values there is probably none capable of being so satisfying as religion. To people who are uneasy and unhappy because of internal conflicts, the Group offers a way of life which serves the person as an integrating principle and supplies the techniques and motivating power to make this a reality. It tells people that their business in life is to follow God's plan—which usually means working for the Group, though it often carries over to activities apart from the Group. Illustrative is the story of Samuel Hoffman, who describes his life as divided and lacking in drive because it lacked purpose. After contact with the Group he found his vocation in the Church; and all his purposes, energies, and interests were lifted to a higher plane by means of this new direction.

Closely allied to the need for integration is the desire that, to some extent, all people feel for an authority to command one's loyalty as well as give direction. "Oh that I knew where I might find Him!" cries Mendelssohn's Elijah, and in substance all of us utter the same cry whether in a religious context or merely a secular one. The authority of the Group is no less real for not being explicit, as evidenced by people who have withdrawn from the Group because they have felt its authority too restraining. Like that of all religious movements, the authority of the Group may be simply an easy refuge from despair and mental confusion. Theoretically, Guidance comes in solitude to the individual, but the method is often that of group guidance, while the sameness of slogans and the similarity of thinking suggest that the source of inspiration often lies in the leadership rather than in God. However, this craving for authority may be satisfied in a deeper sense. What is called "surrender to God," at its best, is an obedience to the authority of the individual's own deepest insights, which may be felt as a real authority. This type of insight is by no means easy or shallow, yet the moral imperative which it produces provides an authority which may profoundly satisfy this need for direction. This gives rise to what many call the "challenge" of the Oxford Group, which is simply a recognition as the final authority of the moral imperative of the deepest intuition a person possesses.

The social psychologist W. I. Thomas lists as one of the fundamental cravings of human nature the Wish for New Experience. The extent to which the Group fills this basic human need helps to explain both its success and its failures. We have seen how the urge to travel has always characterized Dr. Buchman, and his restless journeyings from place to place has been a prototype for the movement. Consequently we can see that new experience in its most patent form of travel generates an excitement that satisfies in one way this universal urge. However, the Group satisfies this need in more subtle ways. The experience of conversion, the making of new friends, the delight of discovering new powers within one, and of building new relations with enemies and friends alike; all these provide experience that is not only new but highly exciting as well. But this same excitement that is so great a factor in the successes of the Group, indulged in for its own sake, often runs thin, as it did in the instance of most of our Negative cases. The Group has more than once revisited the scene of a former triumph only to find its enthusiastic supporters of a few years before interested in other things. Lured by the desire of appealing at all costs, the Group often has allowed its program to become merely exciting, and this feature of its work, which is one of its strengths, is at the same time one of its glaring weaknesses.

Finally, there is no doubt that the Group appeals to many simply on the basis of people's desire for social prestige. Names of the rich and the powerful and the socially prominent are featured in every issue of the *New World News,* if any particular documentation is thought to be needed of the fact that it is the policy of the Group to flaunt such supporters in the faces of all. Buchman has often stated that it is the "up-and-outs" who are in the most need of evangelization, and while one cannot deny this declaration nor quarrel with the obvious fact that the emphasis opens many doors to the Lord which might otherwise remain closed, nevertheless the sordid truth is that snob appeal is part of the Group's stock in trade.

Thus we see that the Group's appeal is manifold and varied; and that it satisfies some of the most pervading psychological hungers of human nature is clear. The picture may be a mixed one, but most of these hungers are legitimate, and though there are secular elements and more unworthy aspects than we could wish, nevertheless we must acknowledge that the Group's answer to the soul's cry for nourishment is mainly a religious one.

Chapter Twenty

What Can We Learn from the Group?

Almost any human phenomenon can be an object lesson if one is disposed to look for the lesson, and so our concluding chapter will point morals at the same time that it summarizes. For we can learn from the Group's weakness as well as its strength, from its failures as well as from its successes.

Its first lesson is for the churches, particularly those which minister to the so-called upper classes, for in every country this has been the clientele to which the Group has chiefly directed its appeal. These churches tend to neglect the emotional and to rely on reason, restraint, good form, and ritual for their appeal. This emphasis on the respectable has led to an increasing reliance on artistic beauty in ritual, music, and church architecture. But at the same time the churches have been losing their vitality. More and more it is the women who are filling the pews. The Group, through its emphasis on emotions and the will, has recaptured for religion the interest of at least some people whom the churches have lost, and among these probably the majority has been men.

This is not to say that the churches should emotionalize their worship. To be healthy, religious life must strike a balance of the intellectual, the emotional, the volitional, and the social. Through its evangelical inheritance, the Group has laid hold on the emotional, and through the emotions it has made a reality of the will. More specifically the Group has demonstrated the value of conversion experience in strata of society where it has been practically unknown and where the genuineness of even its occasional occurrences has been suspected. Our case histories have made clear what conversion can do for certain individuals. Could upper-class churches become just a little more cordial to the Oxford Group experience of "change," at least to the extent of being more experimental-minded and tolerant of other doors into the Kingdom of God than the narrow apertures which they guard, the cause of a more effective faith would be well served. Furthermore the activism and challenge of conversion, with the consequent demand on vital energies, would tend to appeal to men. The more evangelical churches and rescue missions are able to effect these things because they are not afraid of emotion nor of making themselves ridiculous in this way. But to be thought to be emotional is the horror of the upper classes, and so they gain respectability in proportion as they lose their religious force and vitality. And with their force and vitality they also lose the allegiance of the men.

In addition the churches may learn lessons in fellowship from the Group. The social program of too many churches is merely the expression of their religious weakness. Church bazaars, socials, sewing guilds, and the right hand of fellowship following Sunday service are usurping the functions of more secular agencies, and, furthermore, they are not an adequate substitute for that which will satisfy the spiritual hungers of which we have spoken in the previous chapter. The Group, on the other hand, has developed a fellowship not through watering down religion but invigorating it. Its appeal is not that it makes religion easy, but that it challenges the individual to follow the best that he knows, and it is the sharing of these high and ultimate issues of his existence that enables a person to realize the joys of a fellowship undreamed of by the conventional church-goer.

The practice of silence is another suggestion that the Group has to make to the churches. One need not swallow the theory of Guidance in its bald simplicity in order to appreciate the value of that aspect of communion in which the worshipper is neither importuning the Deity nor supplying Him with a quantity of mundane information which He might be supposed to know already; but rather is making himself alert to the incursion of the Divine influence in an experience of silence. Already the churches have made some rather timid steps in this direction, and it is possible that Groupists may have had some part in experiments of this kind.

But at the same time that the Group underlines some failures of the churches through its strengths, it also sounds some warnings to them in consequence of its weaknesses. We have alluded to the need for balance. If the Group is strong in the fields of the emotional, the social, and the volitional, it is just as definitely weak in the area of the intellectual. Most of its serious shortcomings can be tracted partly or wholly to this defect.

We have seen that Buchman himself is something less than an intellectual. Also he has desired to emphasize the realities of religious experience and at the same time to avoid the dryness of rationalization and the futility of religious controversy. This has led to an underemphasis of the role of the intellect. It is noteworthy that it was the lack of an adequate theology and critical sense in the movement that was an important factor in the withdrawal from the Group of many of our respondents. Arnold Bullock felt that the Group had actually impaired his intellectual equipment, while Millman Davis, after three years of intimate association, broke off because of the Group's "metaphysical naïveté and theological superficiality."

This shortcoming is probably best illustrated in the Group's oversimplified conception of Guidance, which sometimes leads to the absurd dignifying of trivialities, as when God guides a Groupist to be on hand for a business appointment. Much worse, it sometimes leads to acting on unconsidered personal hunches, as when guidance comes to interfere in complicated and intimate affairs.

Then, while the Group has done excellent work in sharpening the moral and ethical practices of individuals, it has seemed ethically very obtuse in certain fields, particularly in areas where its interests as a movement are concerned. The great emphasis on the evangelization of the rich seems a little out of place in a truly Christian movement, while the exaggerations of its publicity and misuse of prominent names seem to have appealed to many as of doubtful honesty. Perhaps typical of such questionable practices is the appropriation of the name of Oxford by the movement. There is little doubt that the prestige and advertising value of the name was the leading consideration involved, for it not only serves to confuse the Group with the Oxford Movement but it obscures its true origins, which are mainly American and chiefly Buchman himself.

This moral obtuseness exhibits itself also in the blindness of the Group to social evil; or perhaps, more accurately stated, in the idea that all such evil can be eliminated through the conversion of the individual. Buchman has said "This principle [of personal evangelism] is the essential of all Christianity and the absolute essential of all progress." Doubtless this attitude owes something to wealthy supporters of the Group who are afraid of Socialism and Communism, but chiefly it is due to sincere members whose thinking is politically or economically too unsophisticated to conceive the temptations that the mere structure of society imposes on the individual. This has led the Group often to be associated with the forces of social greed and reaction. It has also sympathized with anti-democratic forces. Buchman himself has stated that democracy or dictatorship makes little difference as long as people are God-guided.

It is in ways like these that the Group demonstrates the weakness of any religious program that depreciates the mind. Quiet Times have their values, as we have indicated, but the Group too often seems to feel that God will do all the hard thinking while the Groupist need do little more than seize on whatever idea comes into his head. Anything but the simplest theology is superflous. One of the results of such emphases is the failure of the Group to appeal to many of the keener minds, and those that it does interest are not apt to give it their allegiance for long. The churches are better equipped in this area than the Group, though it does not follow that those which neglect the emotional factor are necessarily strong here. Provided that the programs of the churches are balanced, all elements need intensification. The weaknesses of the Group we have just discussed indicate some of the penalties of paying too little attention to things of the mind.

But the Group has some lessons for those concerned with solving problems in human relations. Certainly worker and employer may better solve their problems in the atmosphere of mutual confidence that the Group advocates and has actually demonstrated in some cases. One does not have to agree with the Group's claim that in this way *all* such problems will be solved with God, presumably through Guidance, taking care of the economics of the situation and all questions of individual rights. Yet Group techniques can certainly be meliorative, and bitternesses may be reduced and understandings may be fostered so that problems can be solved that would otherwise be impossible of solution. Would the Group only supplement its prescription of Guidance with the recommendation of hard thinking as well, its program might well commend itself more widely than it does. Perhaps both labor arbitrators and the Group can here learn something from the techniques of the Quakers.

Almost the same may be said with respect to racial and national prejudice. Some of the Group's most moving apostles are those who have overcome bitter prejudices of this type, and so have found the freedom to live more deeply satisfying lives. There is no lesson more urgently needed in our world of today than that of how to get rid of our hatreds. If the Group can effect a change of heart in even a few individuals, it is worth a hearing on the part of those who wish to know how this can be done.

Our picture of the Group has not been a consistent one, and some may question whether the benefits of the Group may be enjoyed without its drawbacks. Can its program operate apart from itself? Groupists imply that this is not possible, and it owes so much to the peculiar genius of Dr. Buchman that one wonders how dynamic a program would be actualized without his guiding hand. Indeed his place in the movement is so dominant and central as to make its future very problematical and uncertain following his death. But the answer is that the values of the Group have been actualized both in quiet work carried on by former members and by other movements whose methods utilize the same universal principles of human nature and the spiritual life.

Perhaps the best known modern illustration is the work done by Alcoholics Anonymous, where life-changing of a very effective nature is accomplished by methods fundamentally very similar to those of the Oxford Group. Both movements have accomplished results through religious emphases that have been possible by no other method. At its beginning, Alcoholics Anonymous owed something to the Group. Yet because of a more humble state of mind, a willingness to experiment and work with others, and strict avoidance of the objectionable type of publicity indulged in by the Group, A.A. has been publicly endorsed by leading medical men and most religious denominations including the Catholic. Alcoholics Anonymous has learned lessons from the Group, has appropriated what has seemed good and has discarded or reversed what has been not to its purpose. It is not too much to hope that other movements may do likewise.

The four beasts in Revelation cried, "Come and see!" and this cry is echoed by the Group, which is anxious to demonstrate its powers to all those sincerely interested in its program. There are many who disagree, saying that its methods are dangerous and that much harm has been done to people who have been in contact with it. Despite our special efforts to discover mental breakdowns as the result of Group activities, we have not found psychological disturbances that seem to us any more serious than might be expected from any exciting experience—for the typical experience with the Group, at least at the beginning, is nothing if not exciting. Weak minds might be hurt by any such experience. On the other hand, it seems that considerably more benefit than harm has resulted. We have tried to explain the Group in order that it may be understood, that its enemies may be a little less intolerant, its supporters a little more critical. But any book must fall short of the real thing, and points of view must differ. Therefore the author also echoes the sentiment, "Go and see!" Particularly when fortified with knowledge about the Group such as this book has given, combined with the determination to be critical as well as sympathetic, it is unlikely that the average observer will receive any harm, while on the contrary he may participate in benefits and insights such as have been recorded in the stories we have told of many who received much from the movement.

The real danger from the Group would seem to be not so much personal as social or political. The preoccupation of the Group with the rich and the highly placed, with the unconscious or open inclination to please such people, is a tendency that is not only sapping the spiritual power of the Group itself but might even lead to the Group's being appropriated by such interests for their own purposes. We have already seen that the Nazis were ready to make such use of Dr. Buchman and his movement. We have nothing but admiration for the emotional drive and enthusiasm exhibited by the Group. The world needs more of such dynamism in the service of spiritual values, not less. But emotional drive unguided by the powers of the mind can become a danger, and even if some of that drive must be sacrificed, the critical faculty must not be put to sleep. The Group must be careful not to sell its soul to measures that, while they are means in its own estimation, may be ends for someone else. Specifically, what are meant are values such as social prestige, newsworthiness, riches, and political power.

But regardless of what it may do in the future, the Group in its past has demonstrated the spiritual life in action and has shown the values for personality that reside in evangelism and personal religion. It has been and still is a real and vital religious movement, which in certain respects has put to shame the accomplishments of the churches and conventional religion. It has been a flowering of the great Protestant tradition with its emphasis on the individual and its willingness to let the individual speak out of his own authority and out of his own authority to follow or not to follow the prophet who is thought to speak for God. But while it illustrates the virtues of that tradition it also suggests its danger, for such are the movement's weaknesses that we cannot yet tell whether it will ultimately prove to be a blessing or a curse.

Yet the Group's real work is still being done in countless lives among a population far wider than its membership, where its results are lost among the mysterious complexities of personality or obscured by the complicated society in which we live. These results will never be exactly appraised, for they are embedded in the most cunning and most secret parts of the human soul. Furthermore they are unacknowledged by the Group itself and unnoted by its enemies.

Appendix

THE QUESTIONNAIRE

Your cooperation will be very useful and much appreciated if you could find the time to fill out the following questionnaire. This is part of a study of religious movements to be undertaken as a doctor's thesis at Harvard University, and is an attempt to evaluate the Oxford Group by obtaining the reactions of some of those whose contact with it was sufficiently long ago for them to have obtained perspective on their experience.

Feel free to omit or amend any of the items using the back of the sheet if the space provided is not sufficient. It is not necessary to sign your name, particularly if you would feel freer in your replies by not doing so. However, a summary of the results will be sent to you if you will indicate after your name and address your interest in such. You can feel sure that your individual replies will be held strictly confidential in every way.

WALTER H. CLARK

NAME .... ADDRESS ....

(Would you like a summary of the results of the study?)

(top of the sheet may be torn off along this line if desired)

I. A. Occupation......... B. Church affiliation........

C. College (or school)...........................

D. About how long ago did you become interested in the Oxford Group (Buchmanism) and through what means?

E. About how old were you then?

F. Were you then connected with any educational institution?

G. If so, which one, and in what capacity?

H. What was the extent of your maximum interest? (i.e. academic, very warm and appreciative, "changed," etc.)

I. 1. Were you active in the movement?
2. If so for how long?

J. What was the approximate yearly income of your family at the time? (underline) less than $2,000; $2,000-$5,000; $5,000-10,000; over $10,000.

K. Was your family background religious? (underline)
not at all nominally average strongly

II. A. Did you *then* feel the experience to be genuinely religious?

B. What is your feeling *now?* (For example, do you feel your experiences such as "guidance" to have been true spiritual influences explainable only by reference to God, or do you feel the whole thing to have been for you the expression of rather obvious needs or enthusiams which you now can pretty well see through? Qualify your reply as much as necessary.

C. Do you feel its influence on you to have been beneficial? If so in what specific ways?

D. Do you feel its influence on you to have been harmful? If so in what specific ways?

E. Did the experience increase your sense of religious certainty? .... The meaning of life to you? .... Zest for living?........ Energies?........ (Add any qualifying comment on the above, if you wish)

F. Do you feel the experience to have changed your attitude toward life in any permanent way, constructive or the reverse? If so, just how?

G. What were your habits of church attendance before the experience? After?

H. Please indicate by check or otherwise how the experience affected you with respect to the following items:

	BENEFICIAL	HARMFUL	QUALIFYING COMMENTS
1. Social life in college or school			
2. studies			
3. vocational choice			
4. moral or ethical habits			
5. hobbies or interests			
6. capacity to deal with your own personal problems			
7. attitude toward sex			

I. 1. Did the movement add anything to your intellectual equipment?

2. If so what specific ideas or training in thinking?

J. Do you think that emotion played a part in your experience? (Underline) not at all; slightly; moderately; largely; completely dominated by it.

K. Were you dissatisfied with your life in any specific ways before you had any contact with the Group?

L. 1.Had your religious training led you to expect a religious conversion before your contact with the Group? 2. Did this idea come to you during your contact with it? If so through what means?

III. A. What is your present attitude toward the movement, its methods and leaders?

B. Have you any other pertinent comment not suggested by any of the foregoing questions? (Use back of the sheet or other paper if necessary).

One of the difficulties of this study is that of obtaining a proper cross-section of those who have been in contact with the movement. If you could supply me with names and addresses of any whose contact dates back ten years or more, I would be very grateful. Please indicate whether I may use your name in writing them.

Bibliography

SOURCES FAVORABLE TO THE GROUP

Except for the first item, all of these books have been written or prepared by adherents of the Group. They supply much valuable information and source material but are little or no use to those who wish to gauge the Group's weaknesses as well as its successes.

Begbie, Harold, *More Twice-Born Men* (New York: G. P. Putnam's Sons, 1923). An early account of Buchman and his converts.

Buchman, Frank. N. D., *Remaking The World* (Los Angeles: Mackinac Press). A collection of excerpts from Buchman's public addresses and other Group documents.

Howard, Peter, That Man Frank Buchman (London: Blandford Press, 1946). Highly colored.

Russell, A. J., *For Sinners Only* (New York: Harper & Brothers, 1932).

New World News. A monthly published by the Group at 833 South Flower Street, Los Angeles, containing articles and current news about Group activities.

SOURCES UNFAVORABLE TO THE GROUP

These are valuable as sources of criticism of the Group, though prejudice tends to make them unreliable.

Ferguson, Charles W., *The Confusion of Tongues* (Garden City: Doubleday, Doran, 1929). Devotes a chapter to the Group; rather highly colored.

Harrison, Marjorie, *Saints Run Mad* (London: John Lane, the Bodley Head, Ltd., 1934). Witty, and a source of anecdotes, but clearly prejudiced.

Henson, Herbert Hensly (Bishop of Durham), *The Oxford Group Movement* (New York: Oxford University Press, 1936). Opinions from a determined foe of the movement.

SOURCES DEALING WITH THE GROUP FROM A LESS PARTISAN POINT OF VIEW

These are more difficult to find. The following are mostly either brief or devote only a section to the Group. However, these are the most valuable for the impartial student of the movement.

Bennett, John C., *Social Salvation* (New York: Charles Scribner's Sons, 1935).

Braden, Charles Samuel, *These Also Believe* (New York: The Macmillan Company, 1949).

Cantril, Hadley, *The Psychology of Social Movements* (New York: John Wiley & Sons, 1941). While Cantril misconceives the movement in certain respects, he nevertheless has interesting suggestions for understanding it psychologically.

Clark, Walter Houston (Unpublished doctoral dissertation) See Preface.

Eister, Allan W., *Drawing Room Conversion* (Durham: Duke University Press, 1950). A full-length study of the Group from the sociological point of view. Extensive bibliography.

Macintosh, Douglas Clyde, *Personal Religion* (New York: Charles Scribner's Sons, 1942).

Van Dusen, Henry P., "Apostle to the Twentieth Century: Frank N. D. Buchman," *Atlantic Monthly,* Vol. 154, July, 1934, pp. 1-24; "The Oxford Group Movement," *Ibid.,* August, pp. 240-252. These two articles are among the best appraisals of Buchman and the Group.

Index

Index

Index